Copyright ©

All rights reserved.
No parts of this publication may be reproduced, distributed, or transmitted in any form,
or by any means, including photocopying, recording or other electronic or mechanical
methods, without prior written permission from the publisher.

This page left intentionally blank.

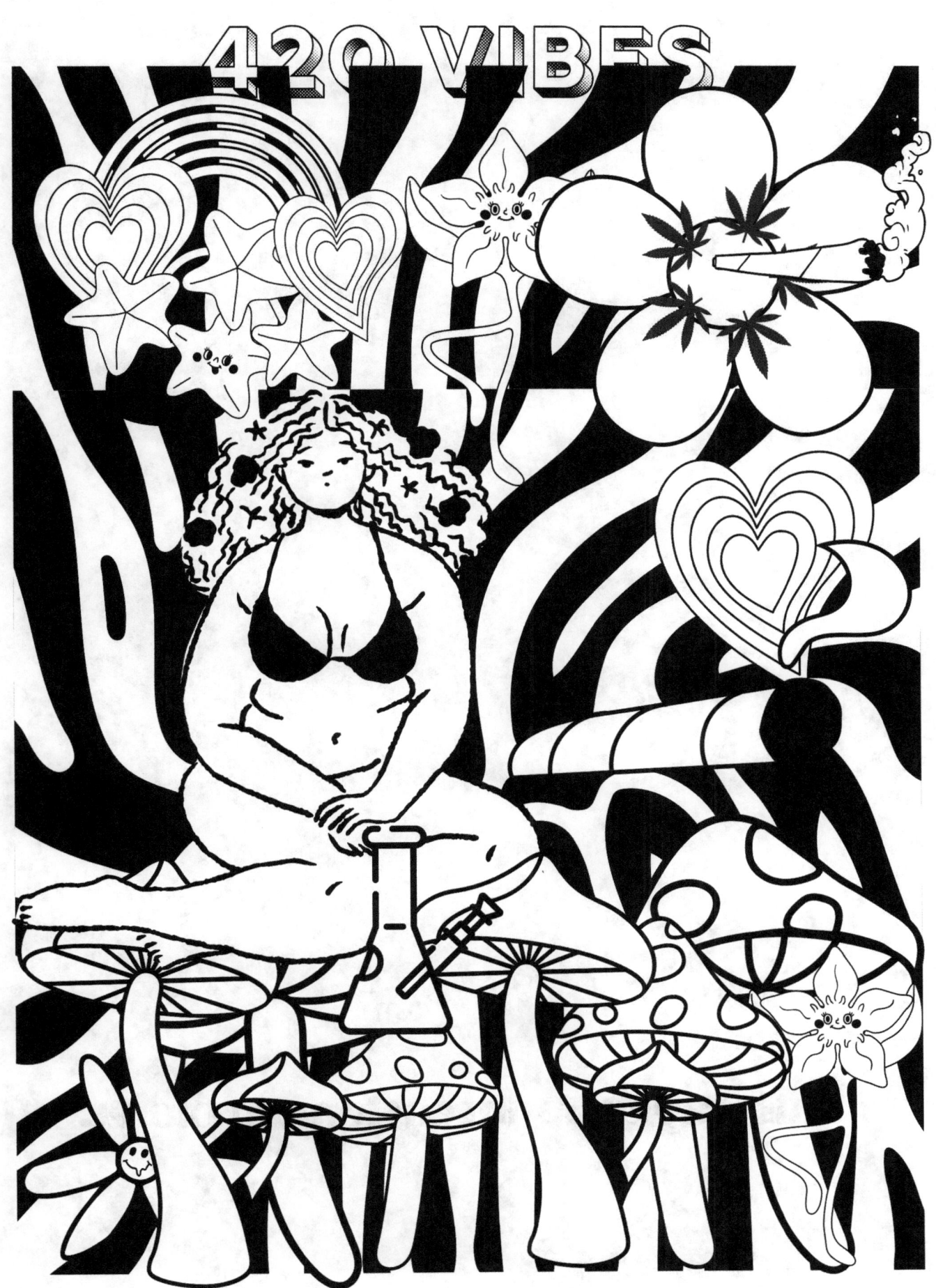

This page left intentionally blank.

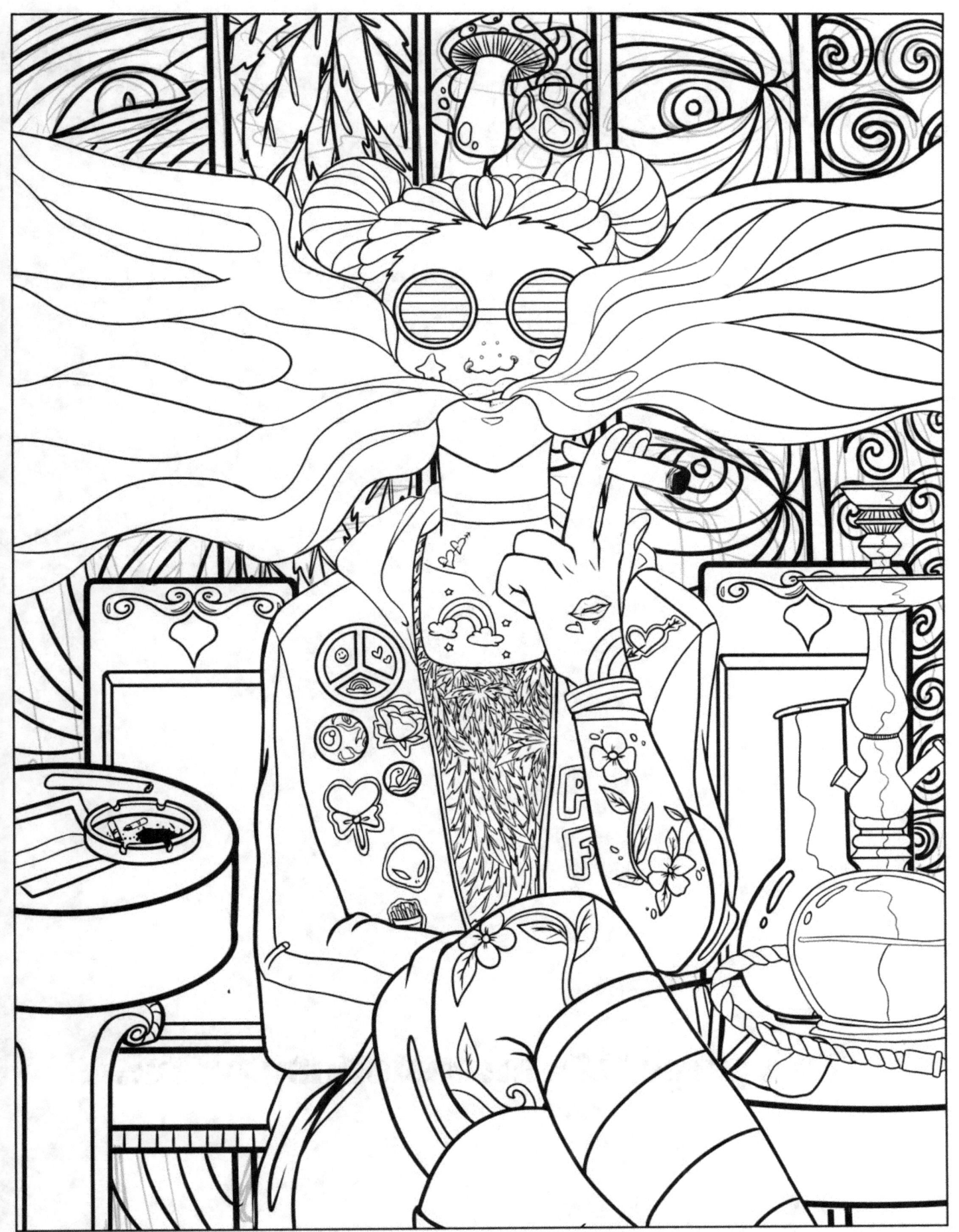

This page left intentionally blank.

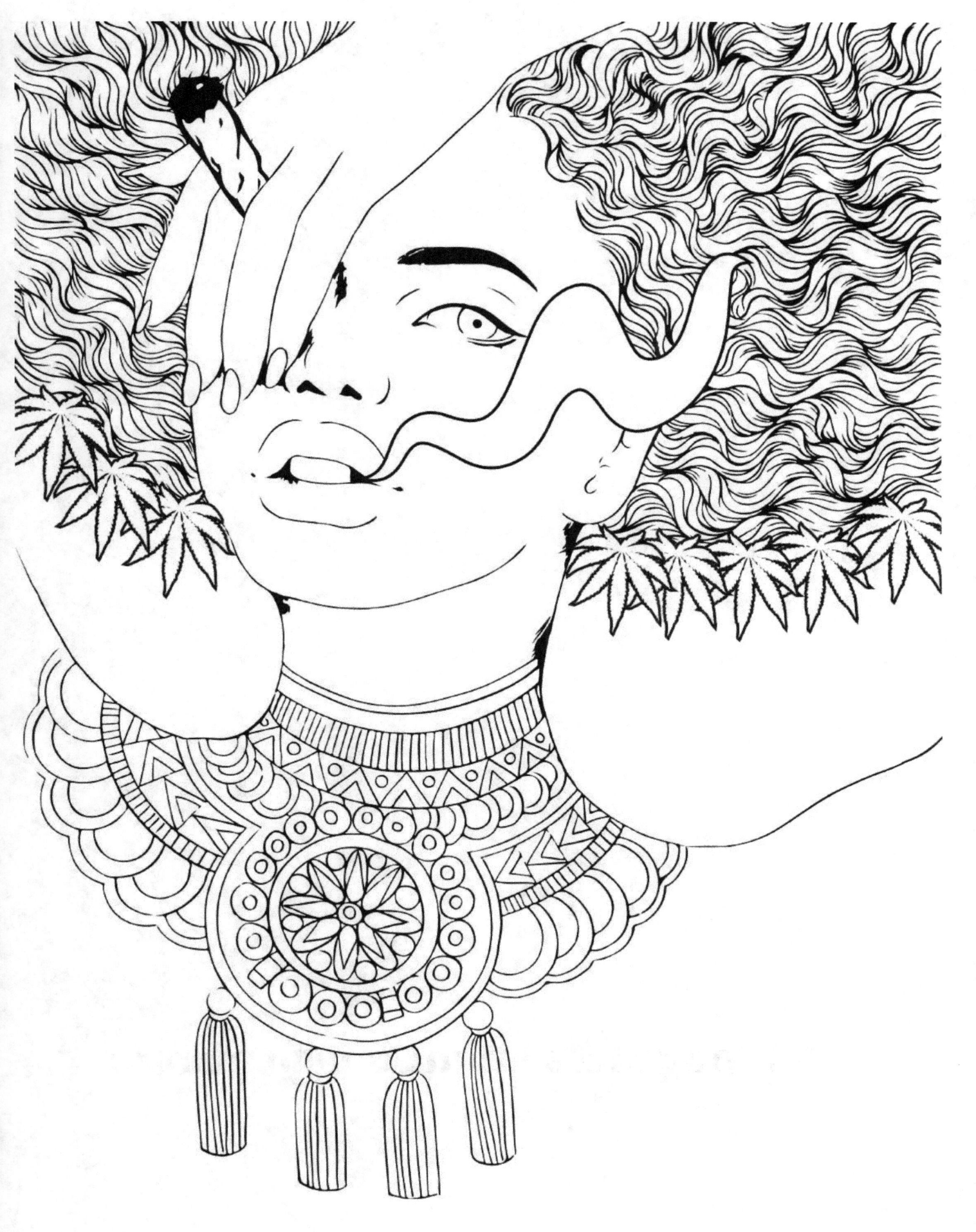

This page left intentionally blank.

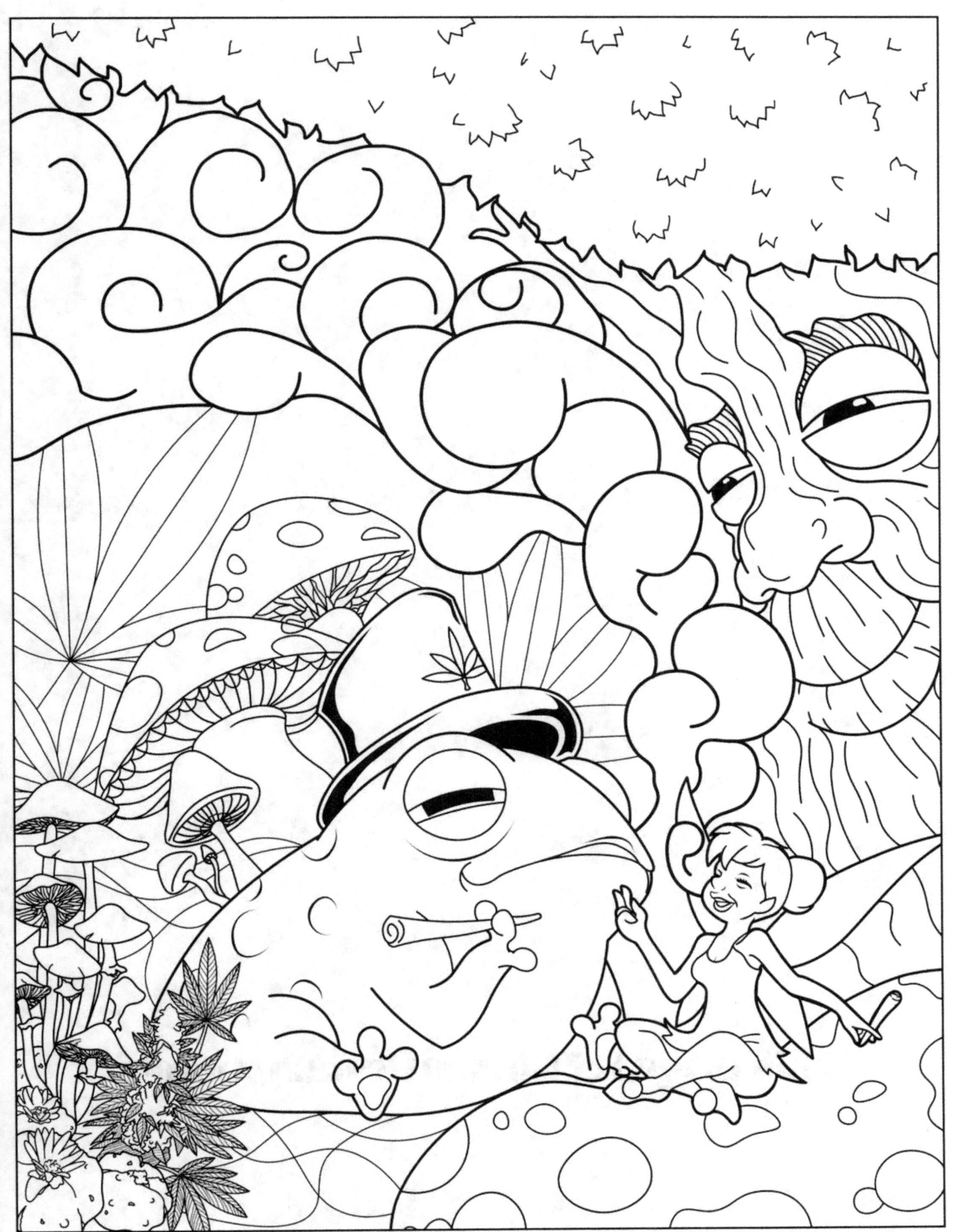

This page left intentionally blank.

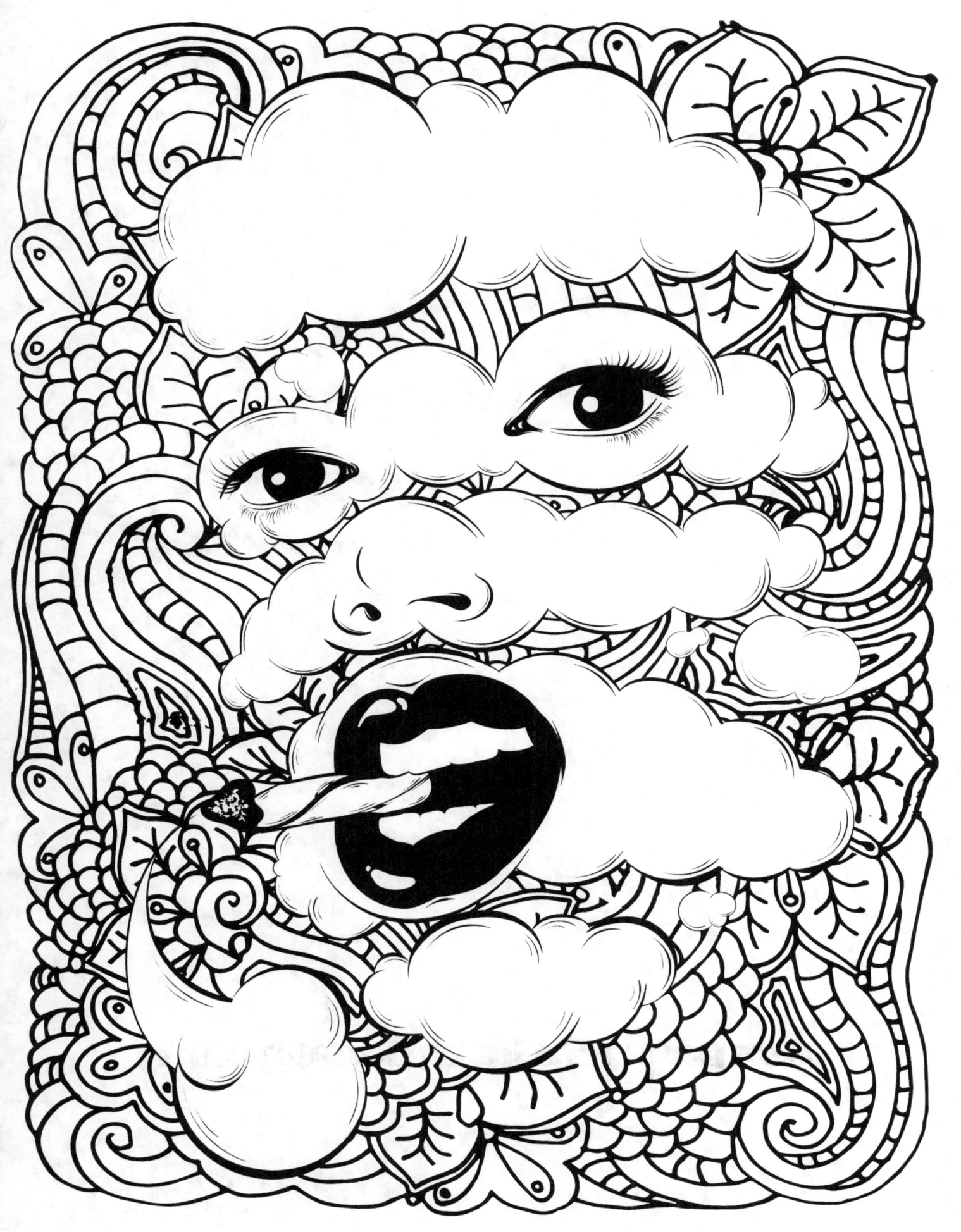

This page left intentionally blank.

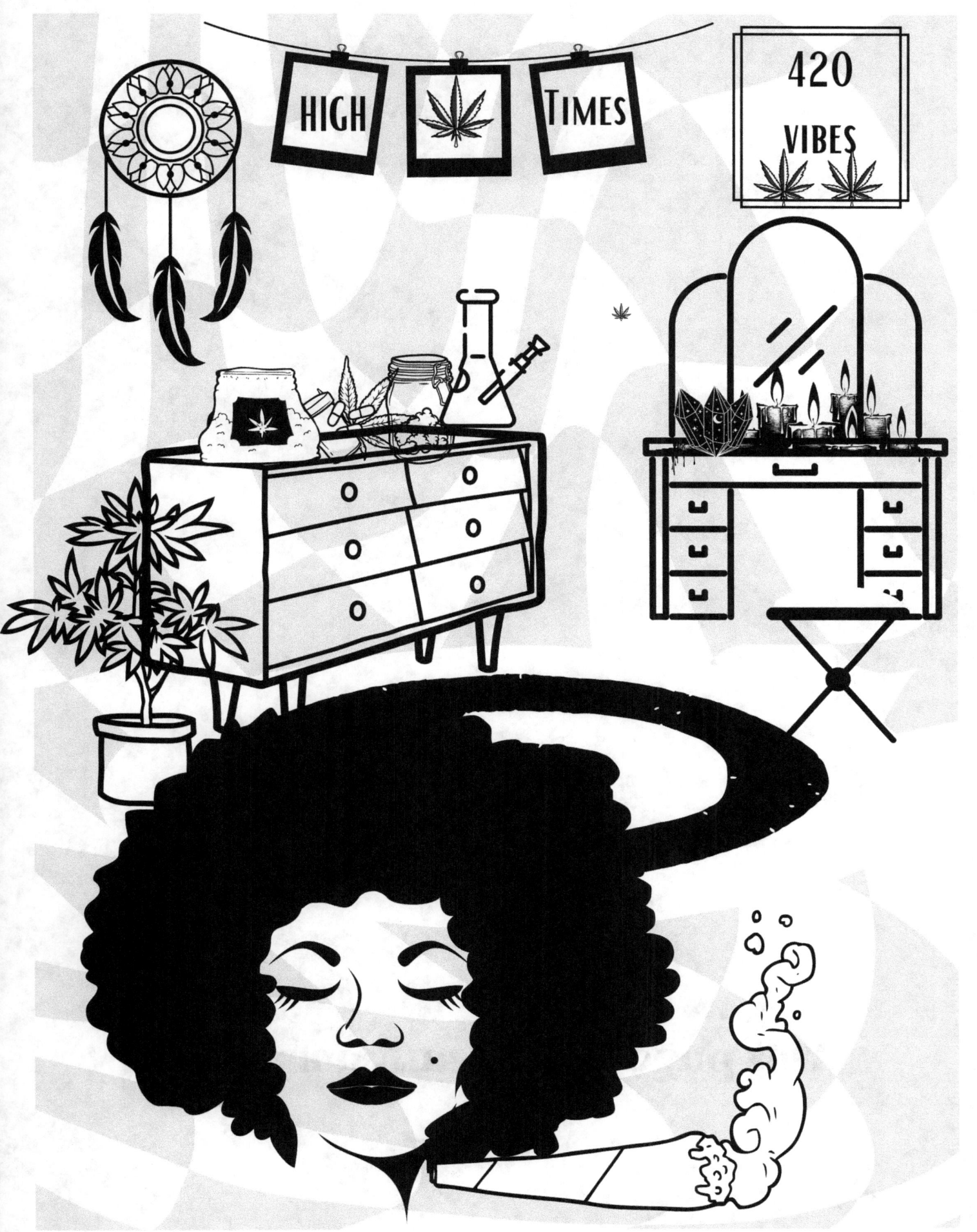

This page left intentionally blank.

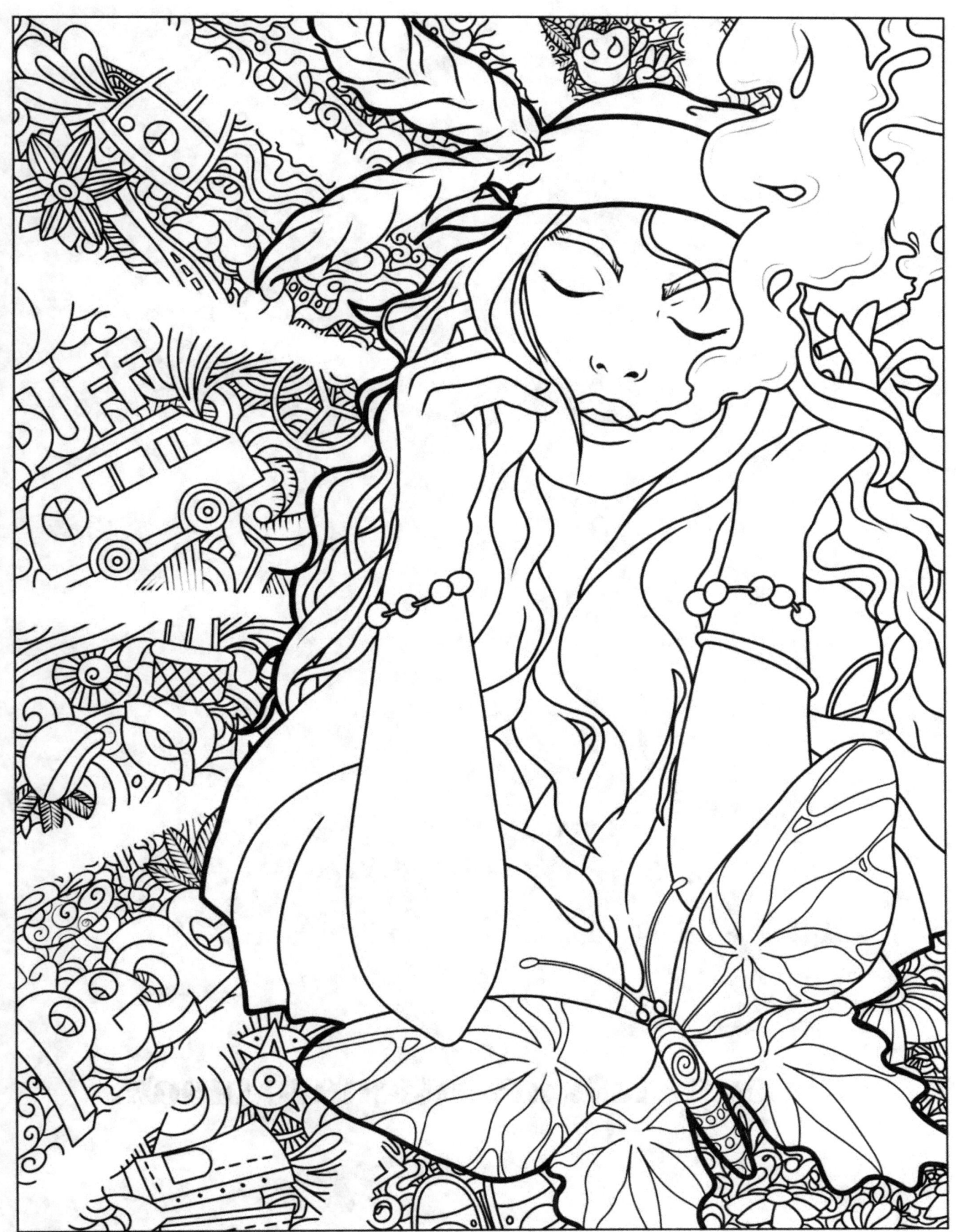

This page left intentionally blank.

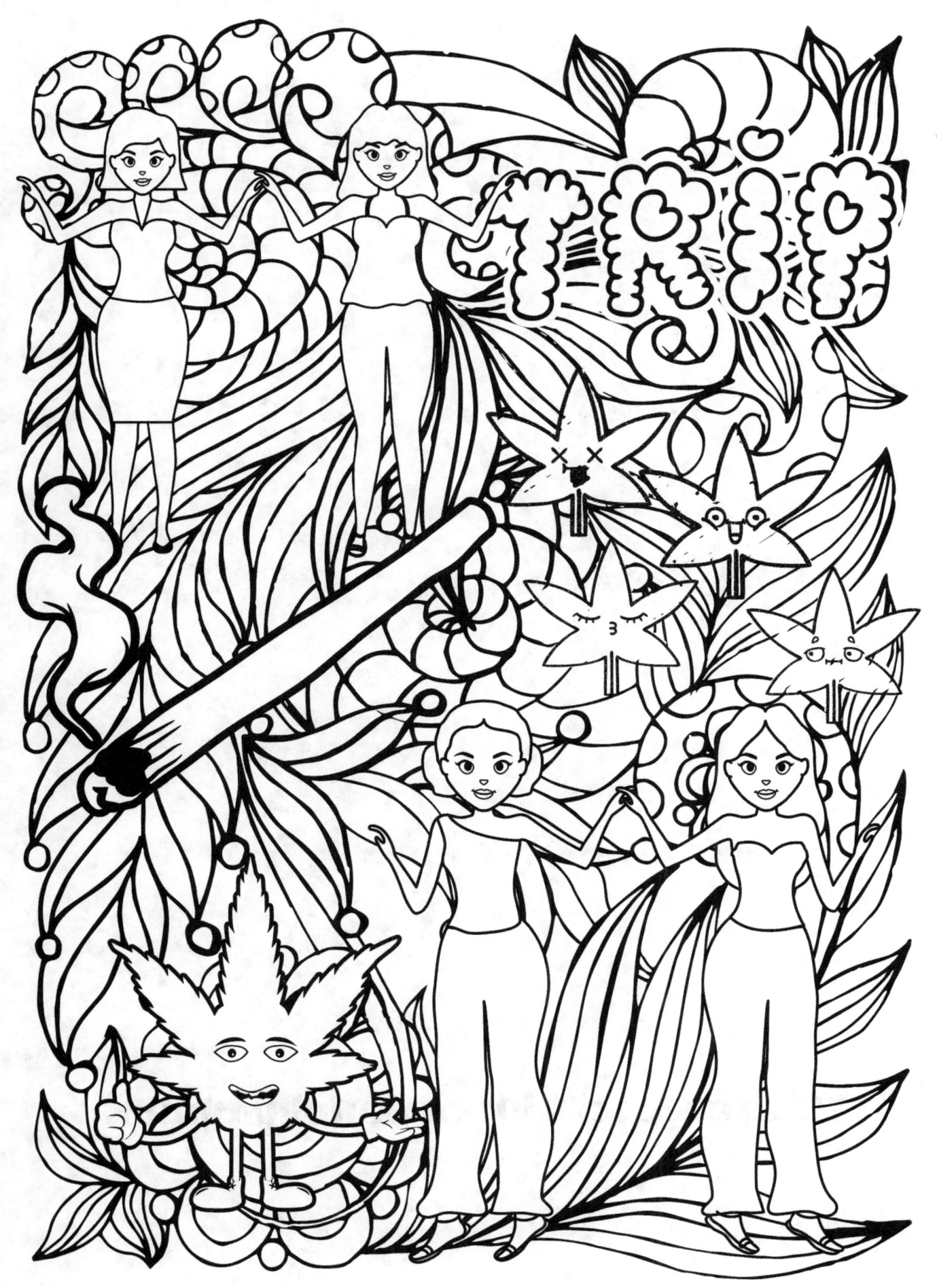

This page left intentionally blank.

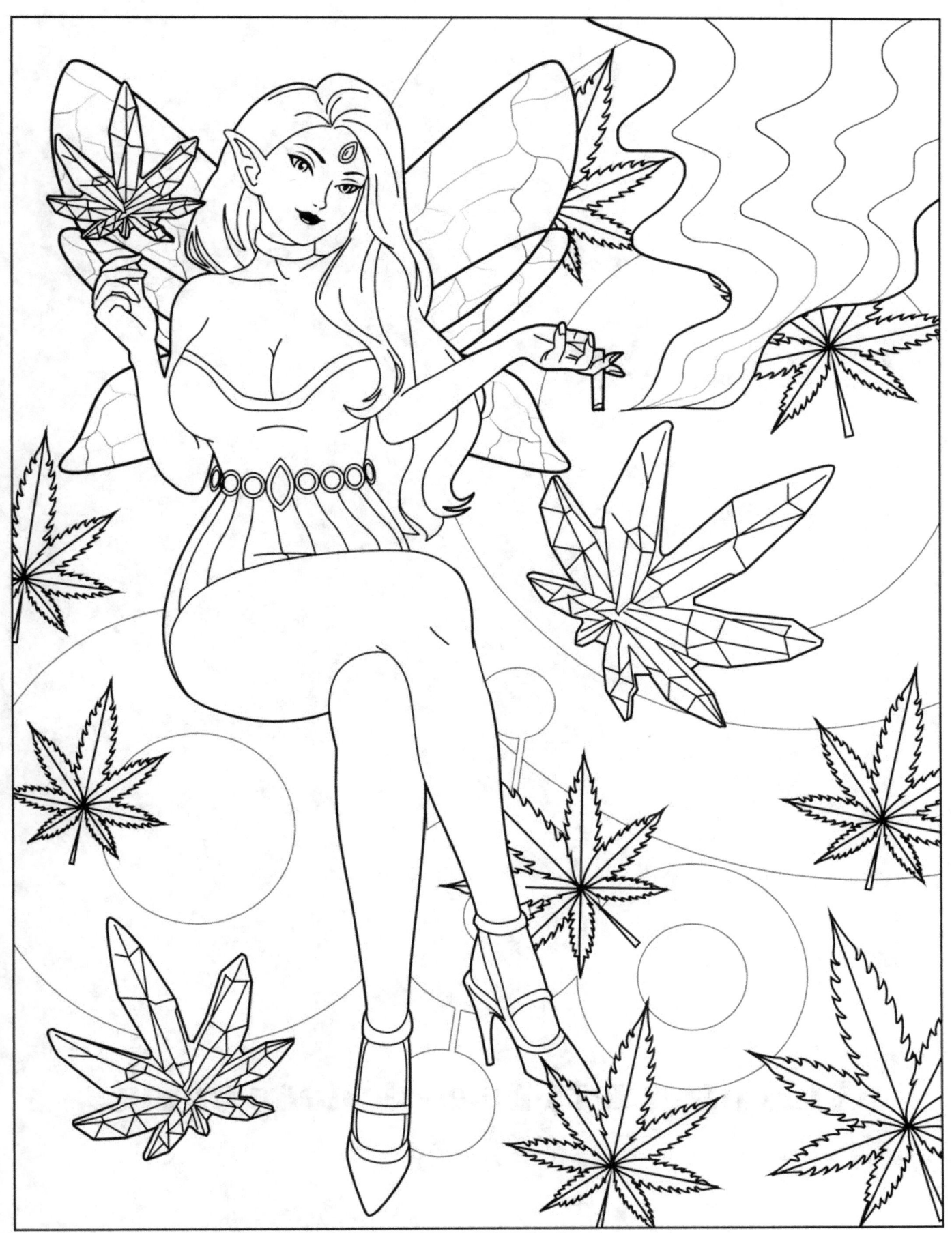

This page left intentionally blank.

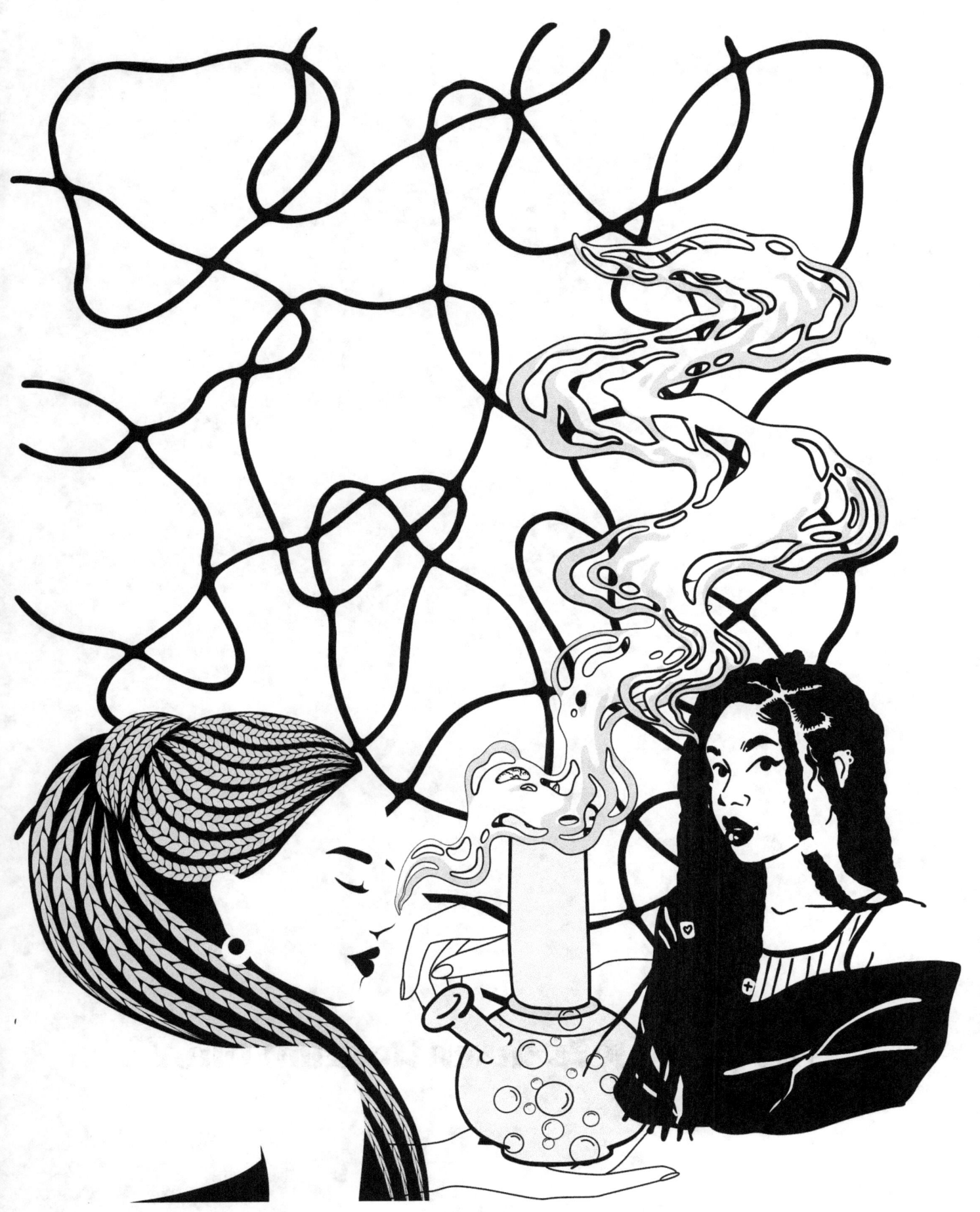

This page left intentionally blank.

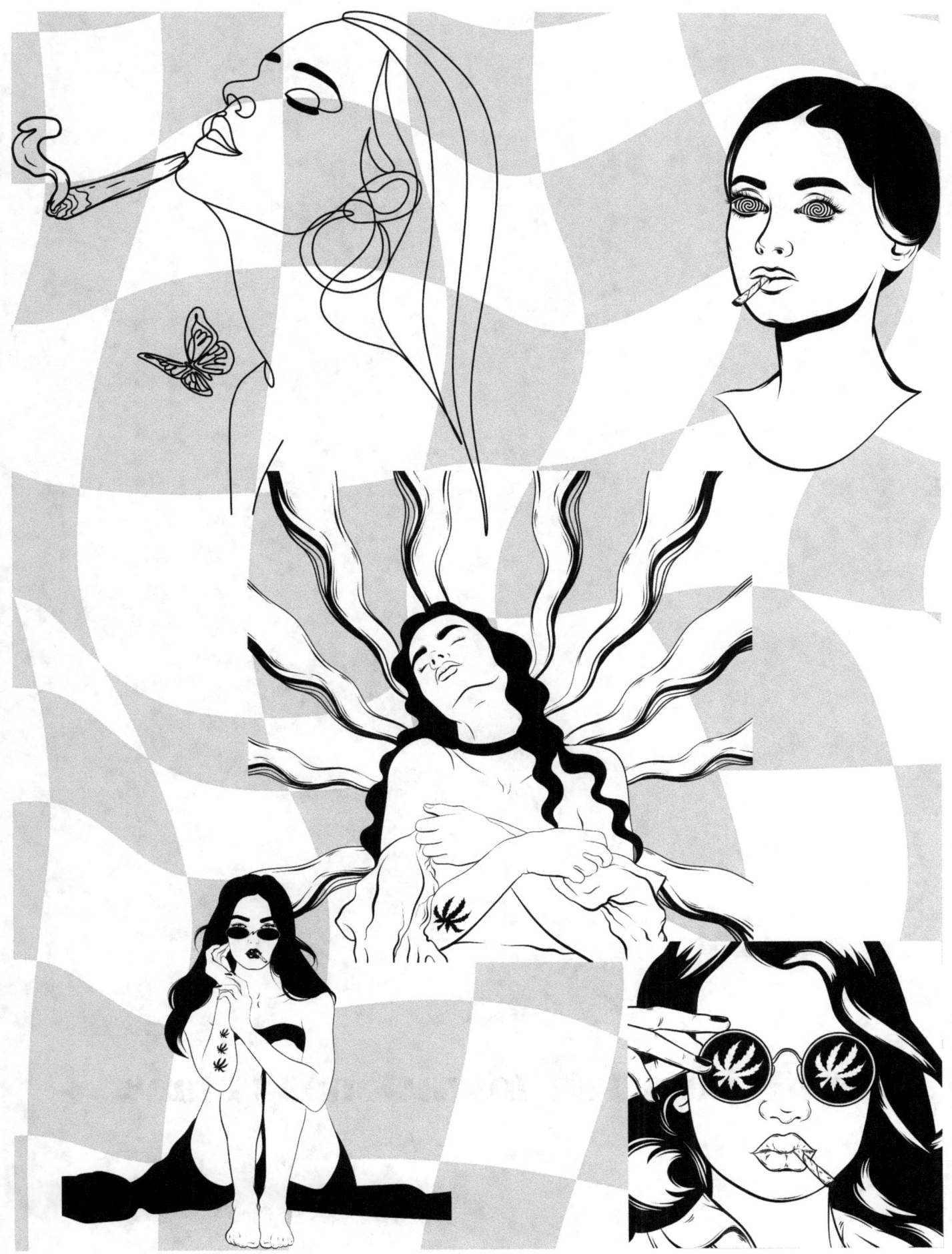

This page left intentionally blank.

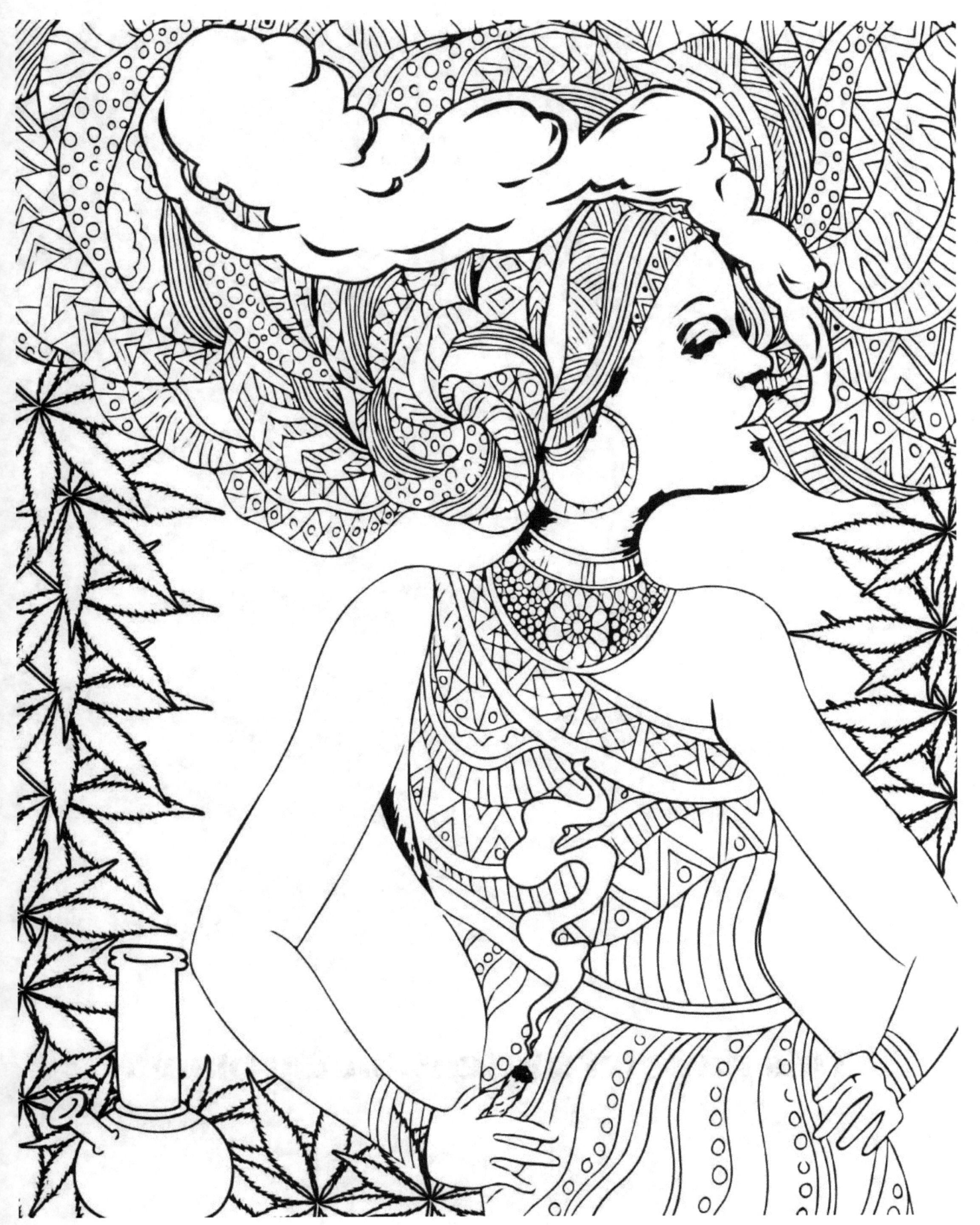

This page left intentionally blank.

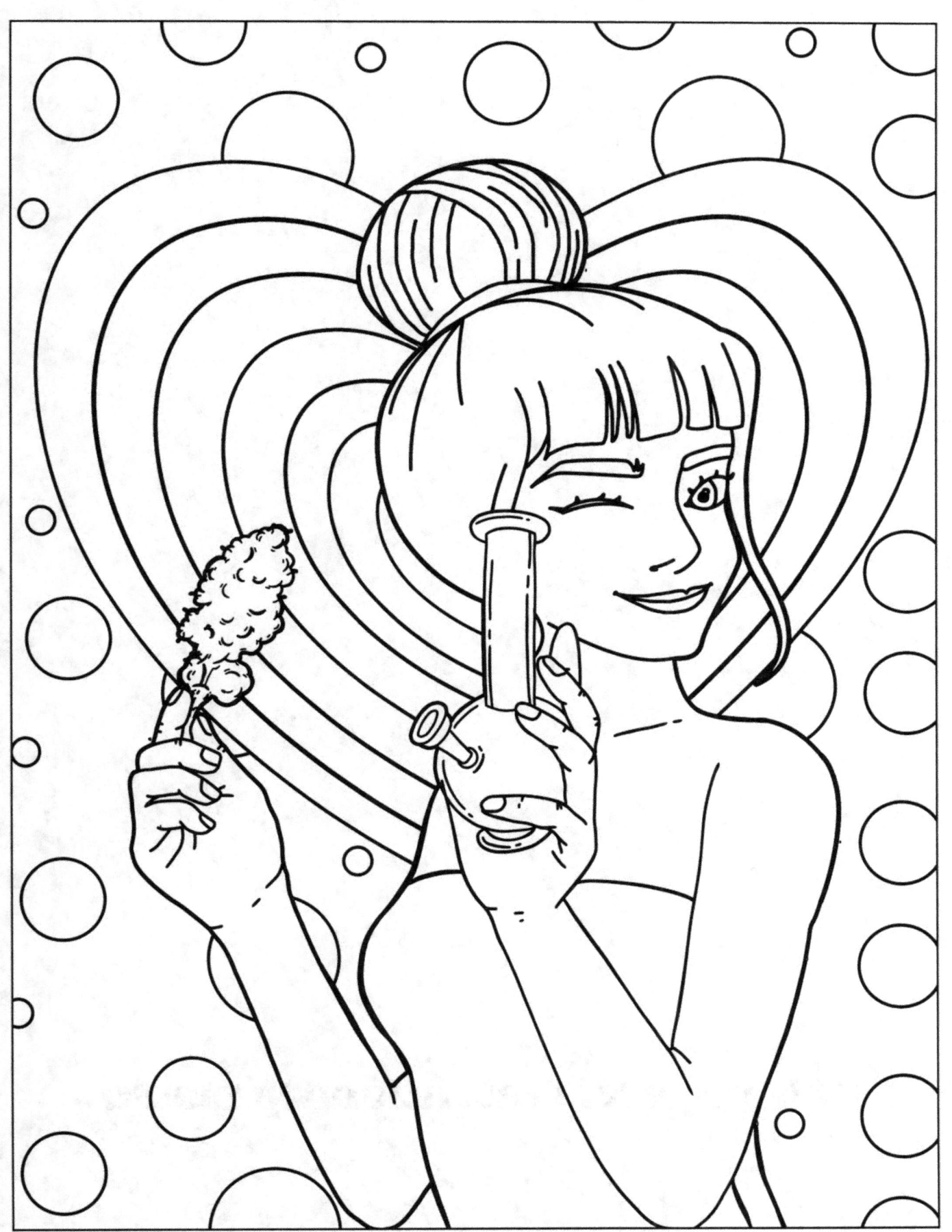

This page left intentionally blank.

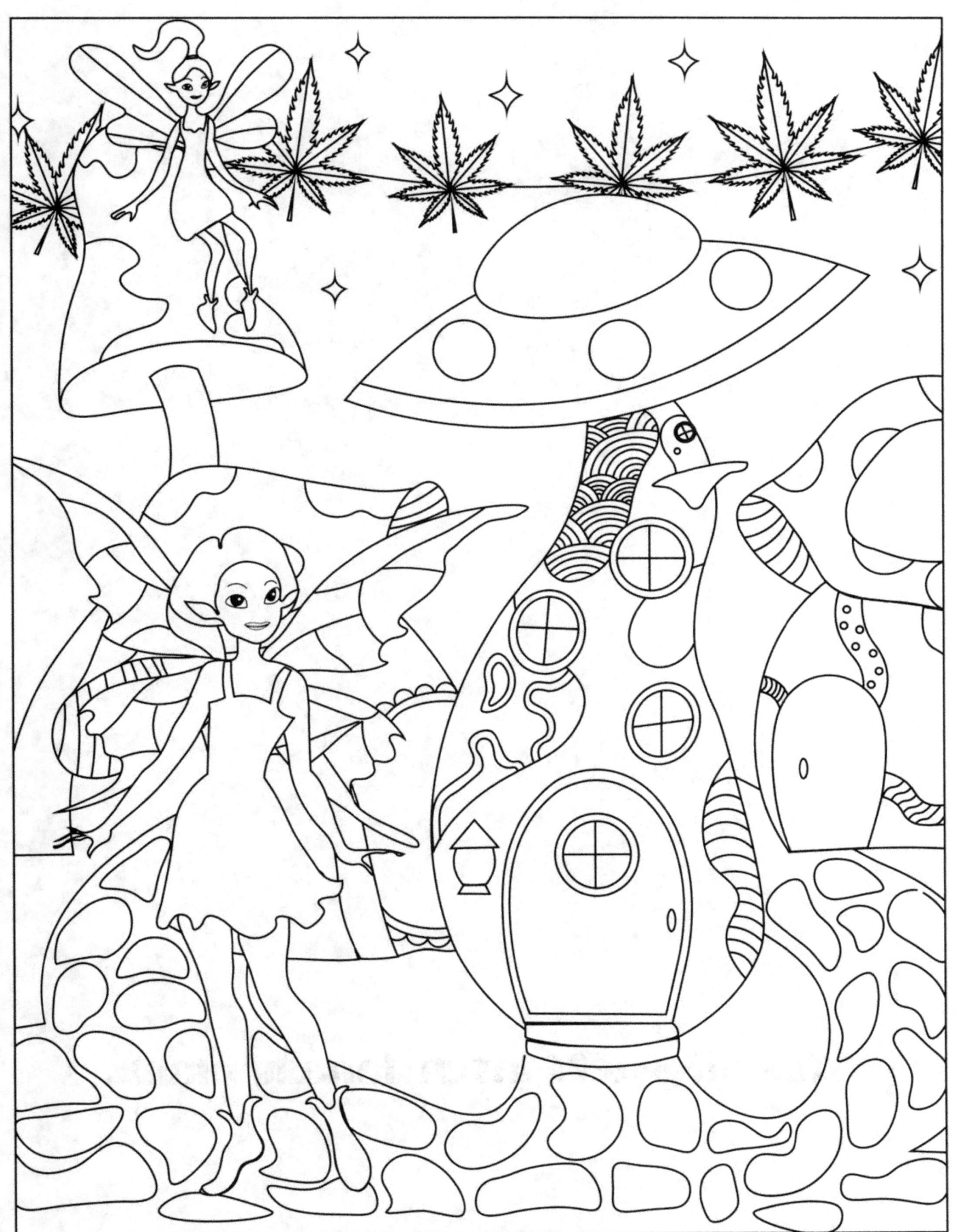

This page left intentionally blank.

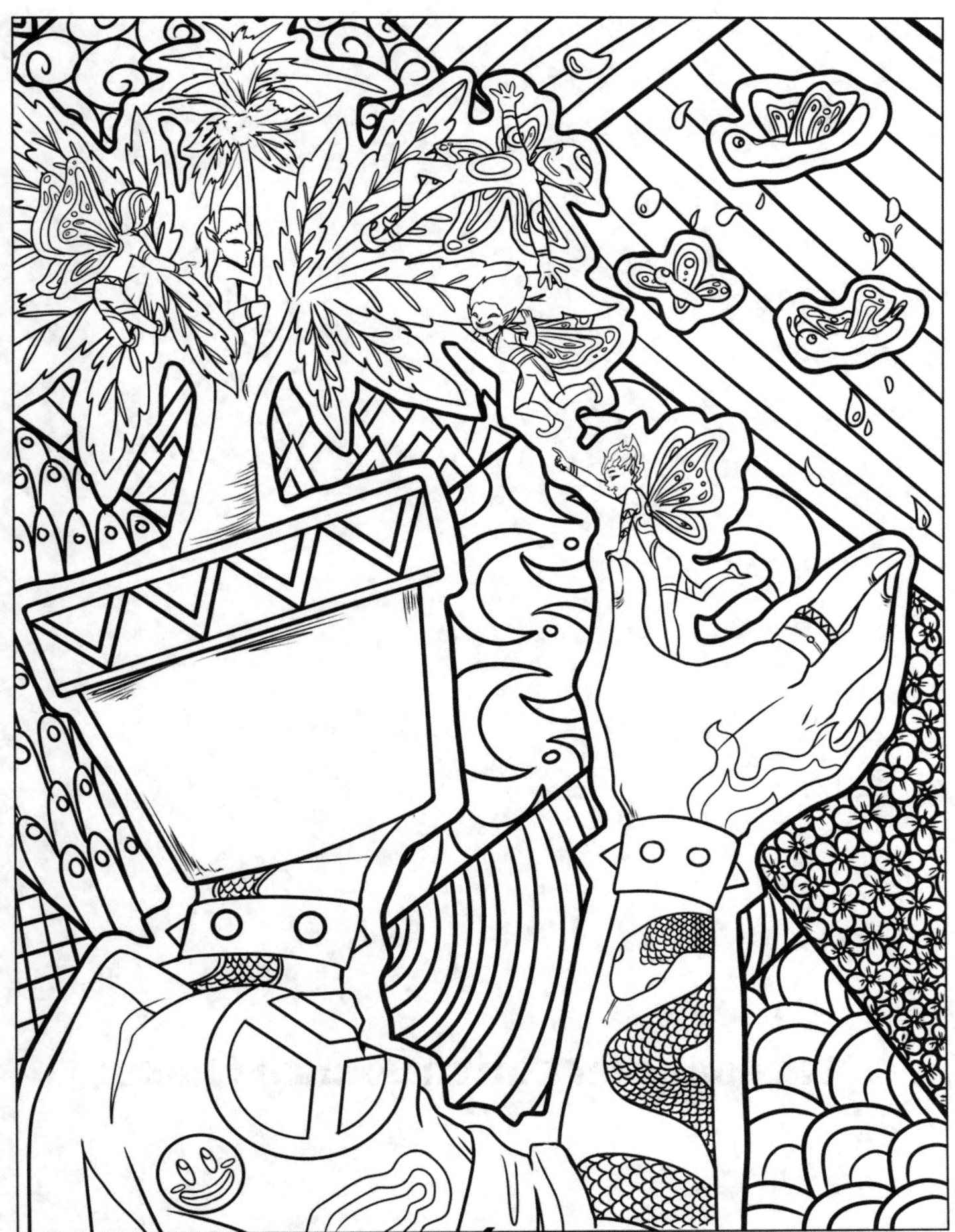

This page left intentionally blank.

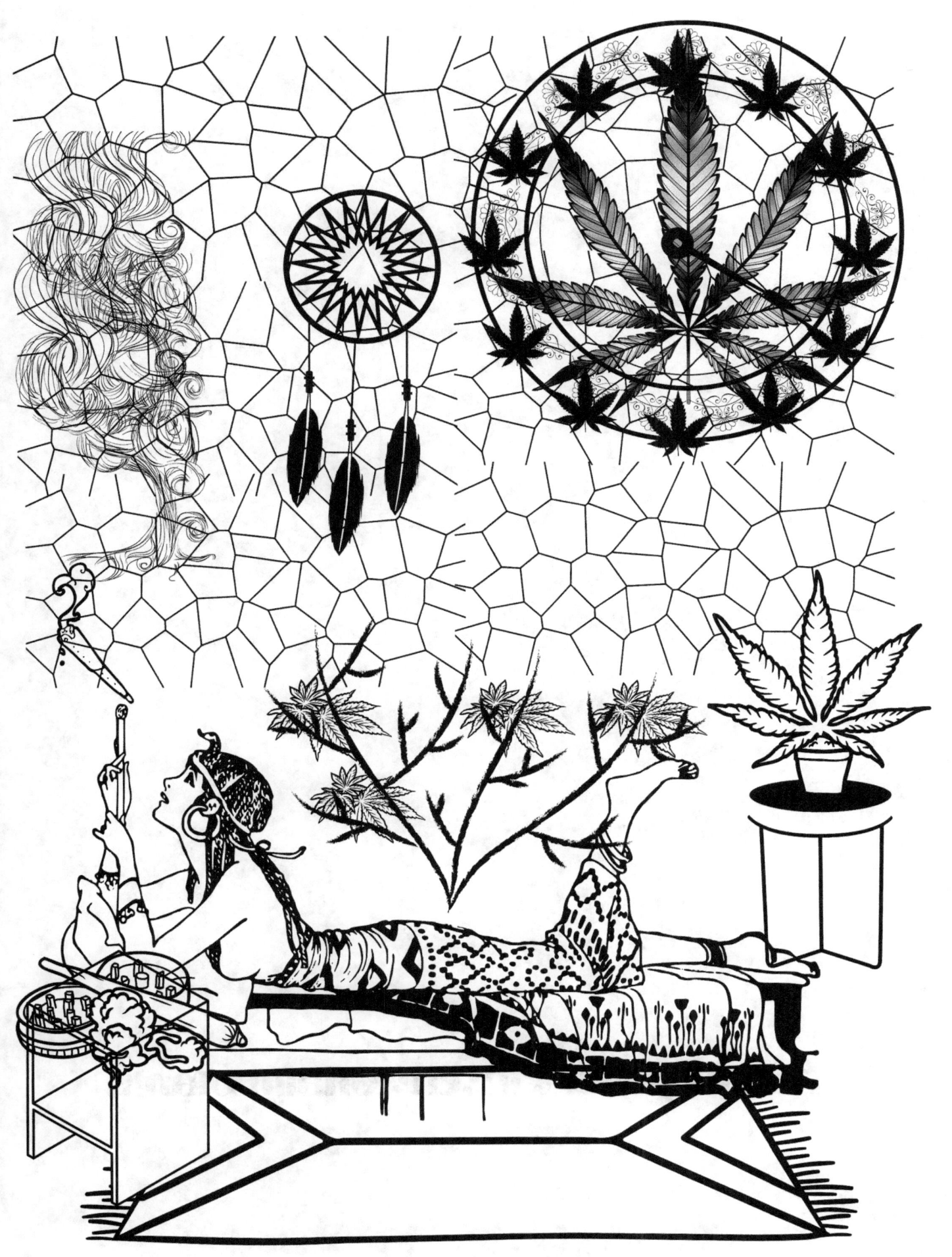

This page left intentionally blank.

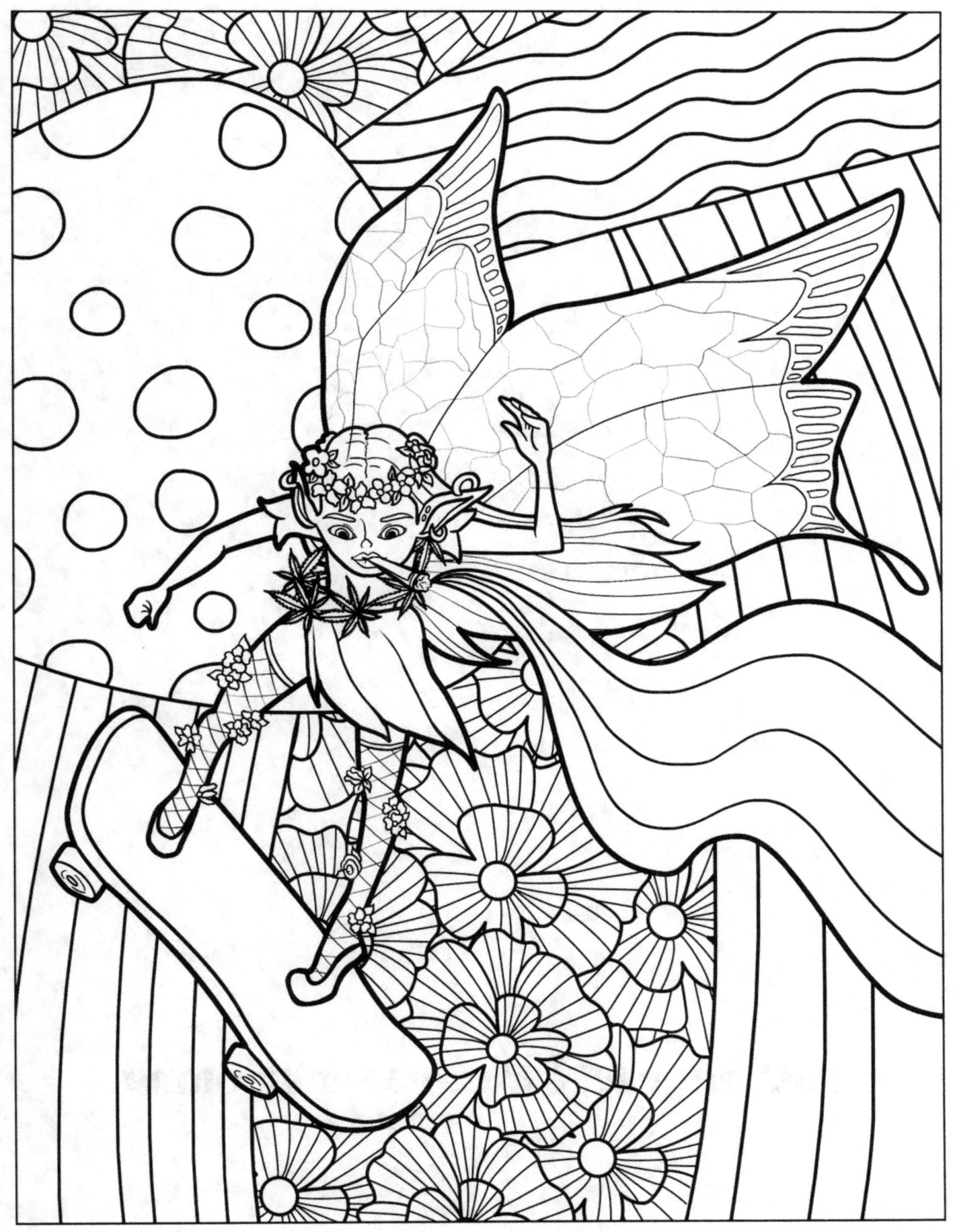

This page left intentionally blank.

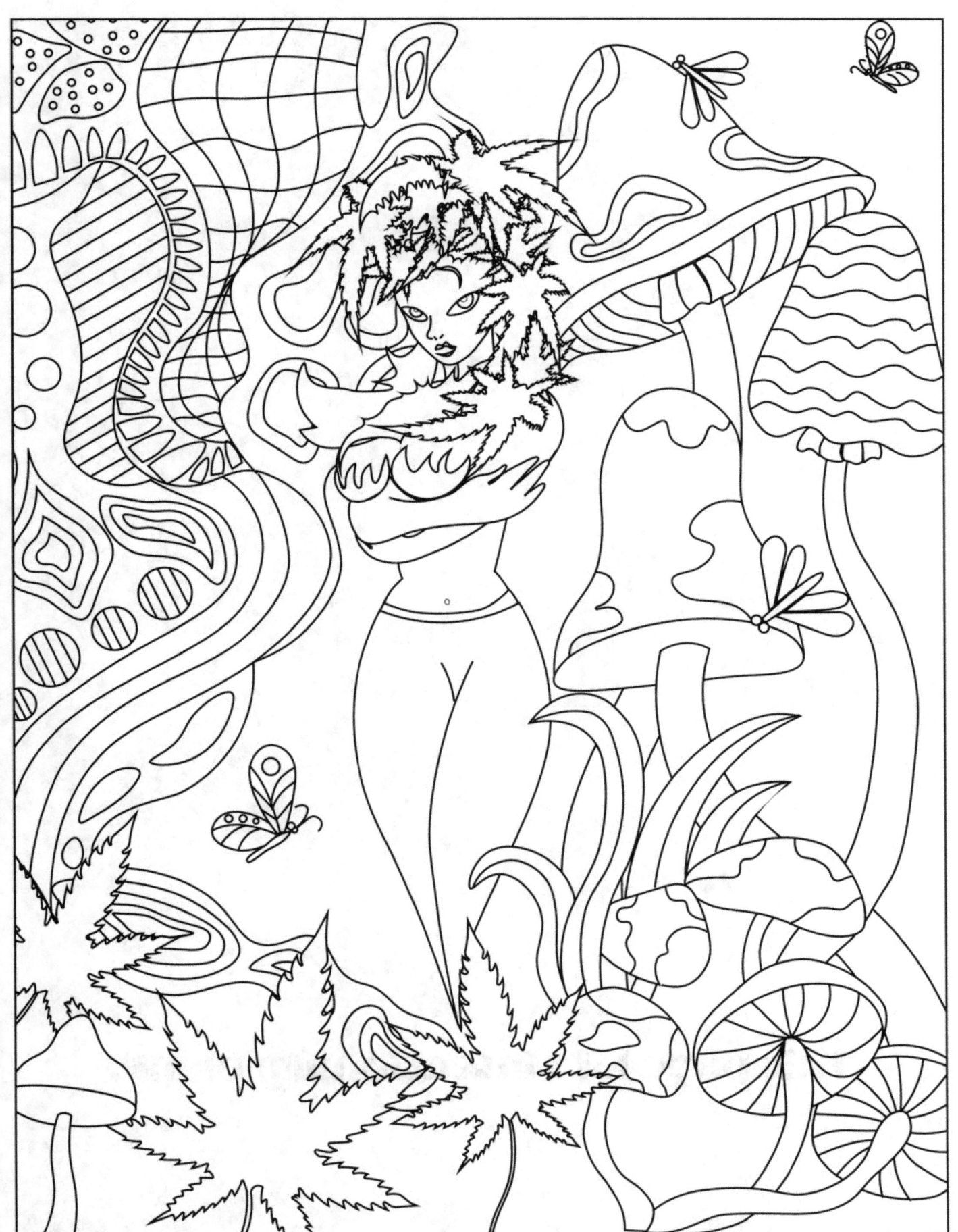

This page left intentionally blank.

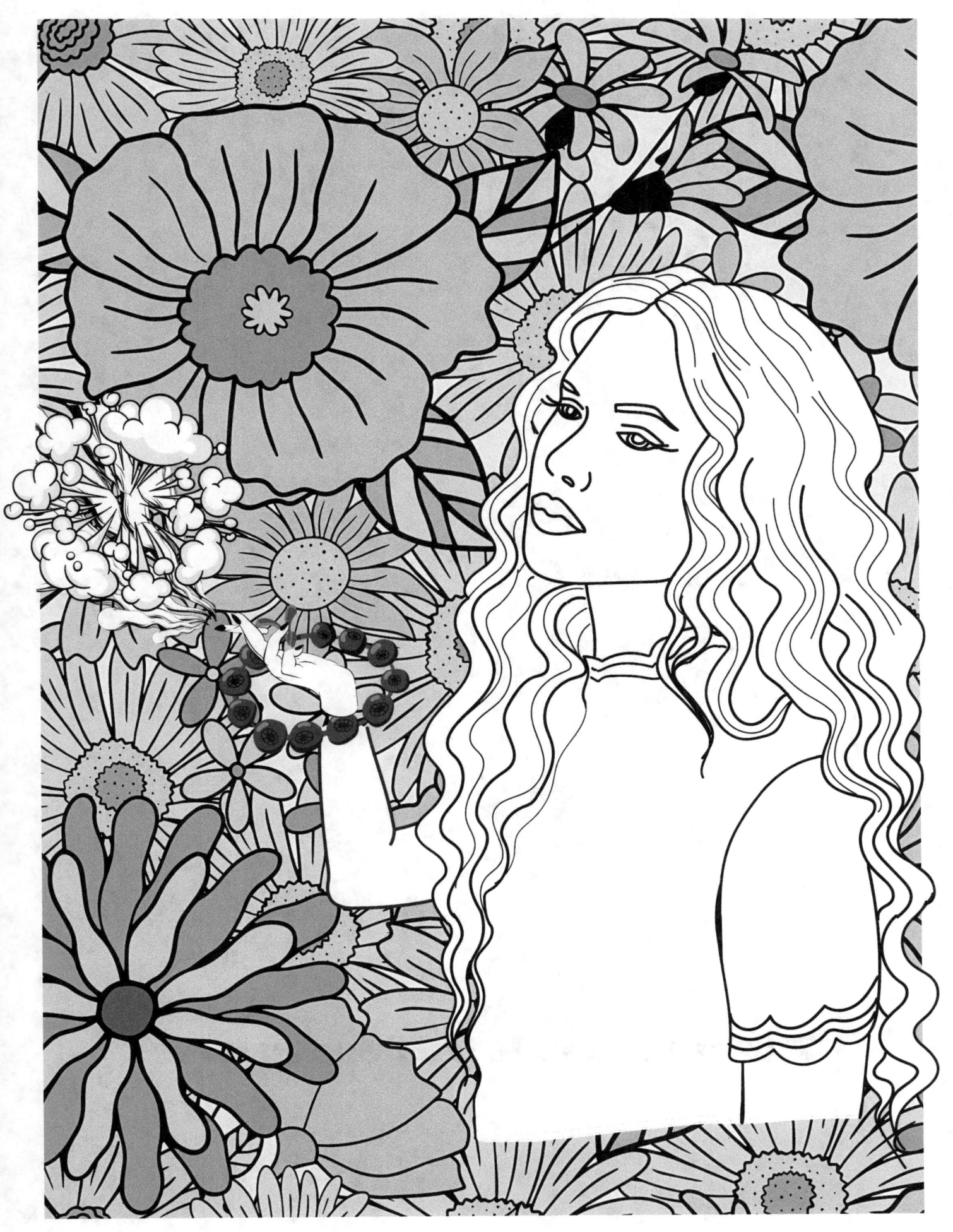

This page left intentionally blank.

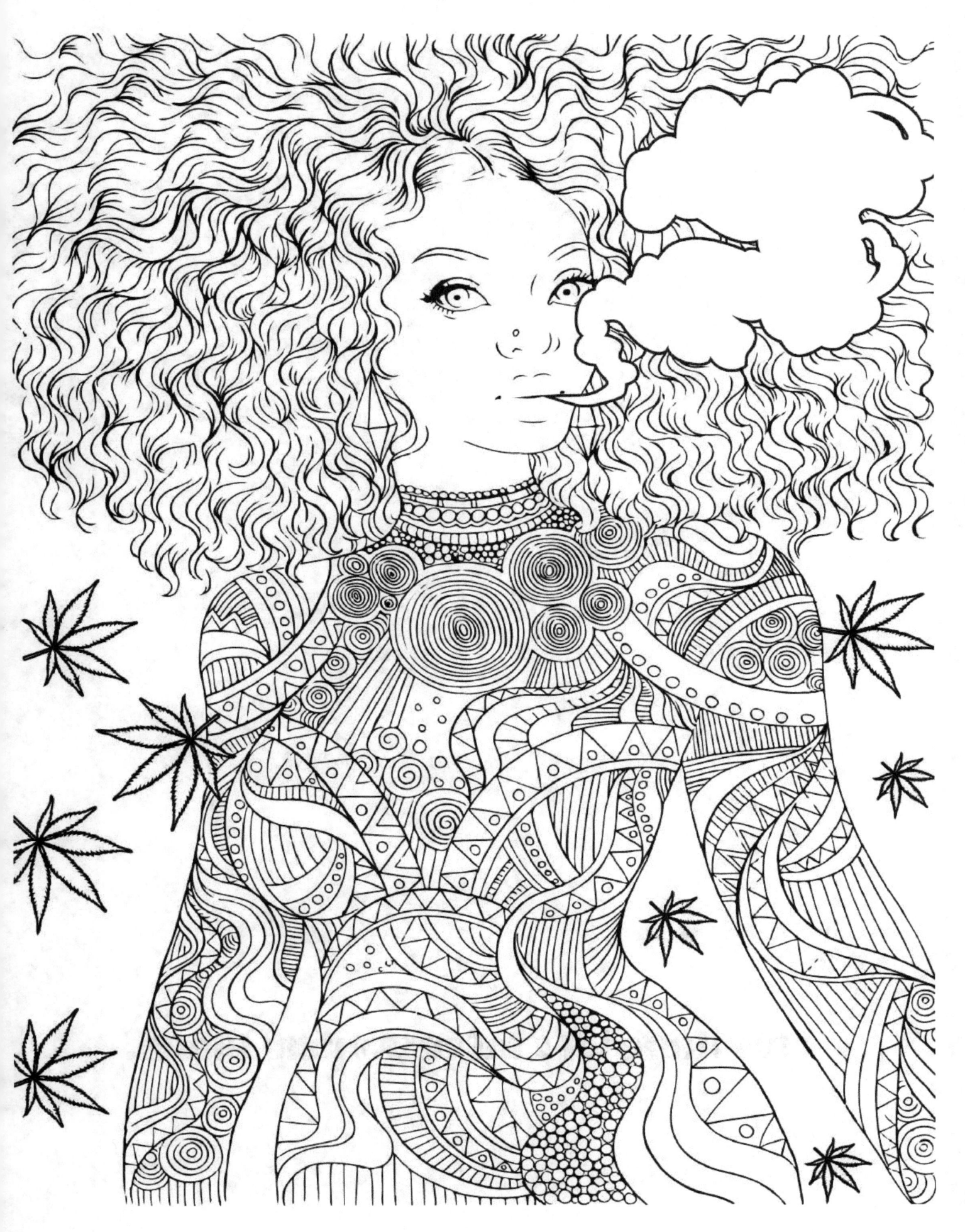

This page left intentionally blank.

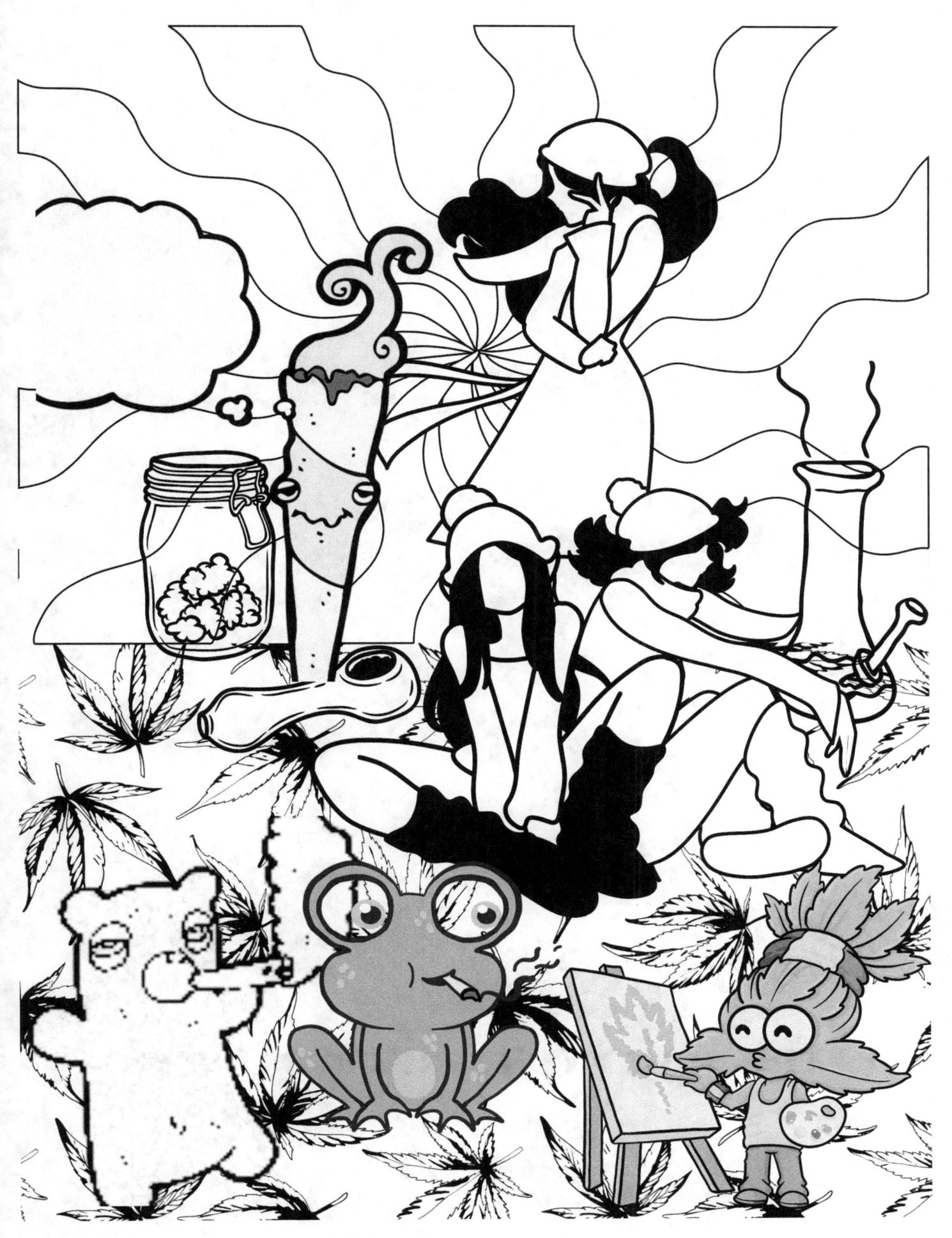

This page left intentionally blank.

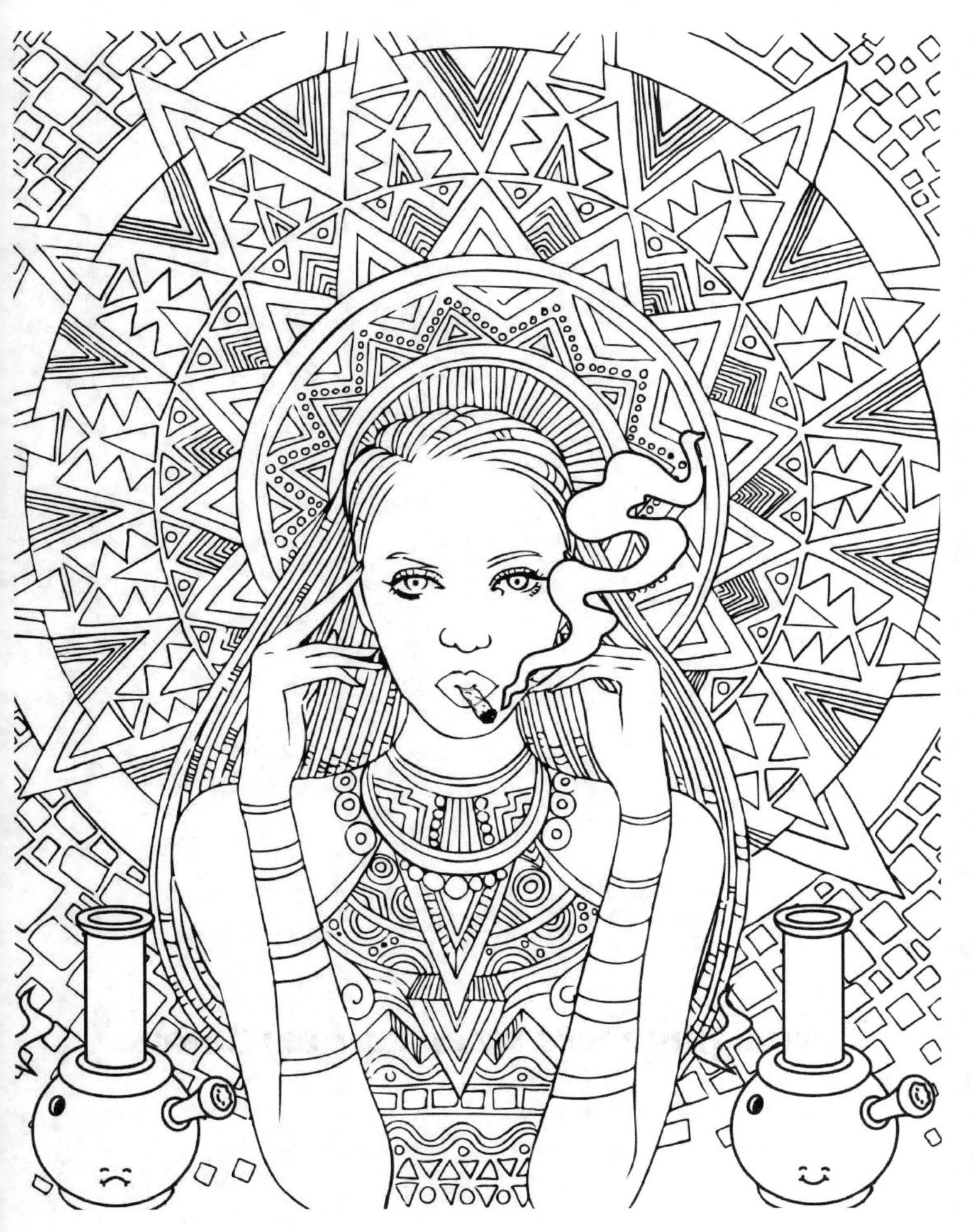

This page left intentionally blank.

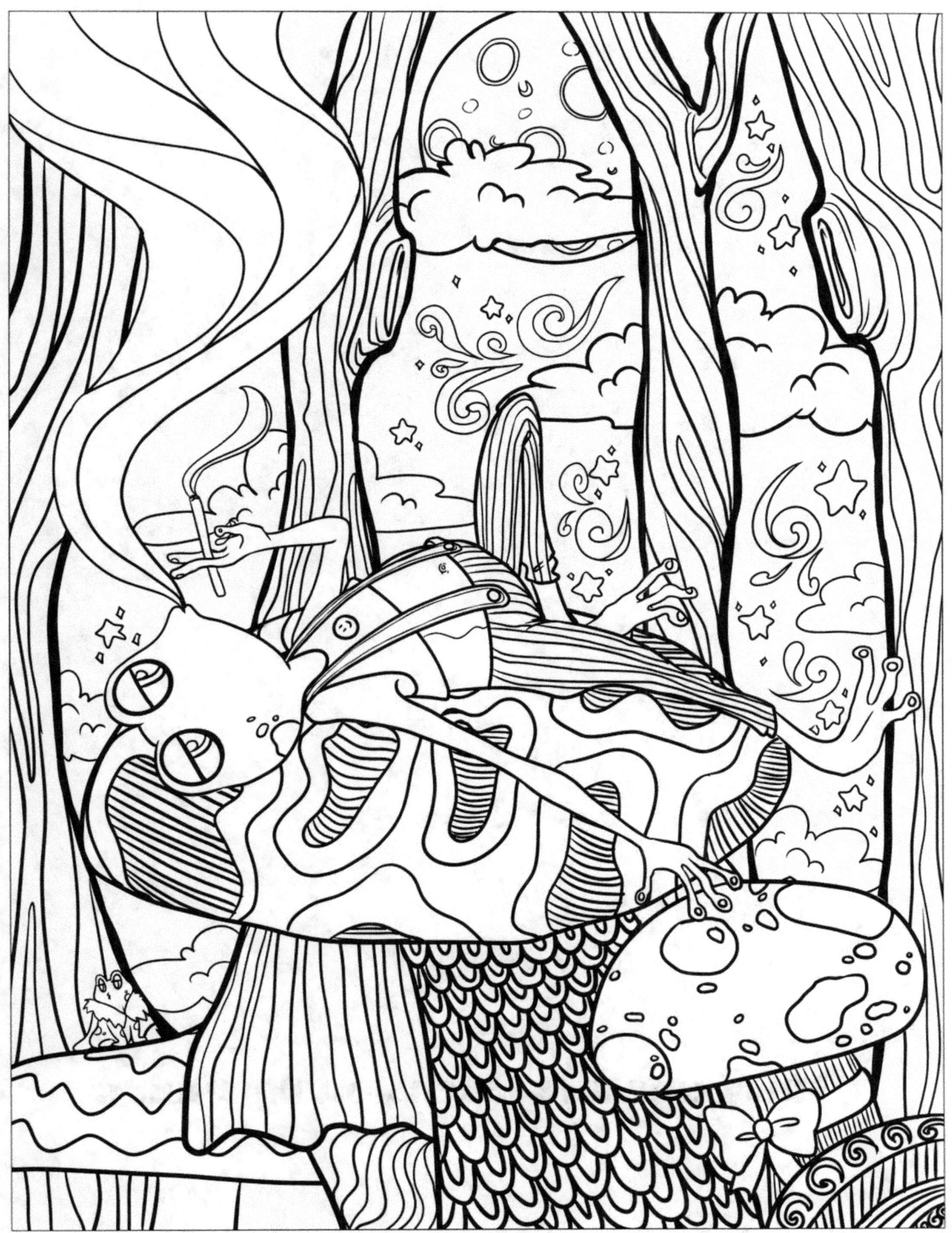

This page left intentionally blank.

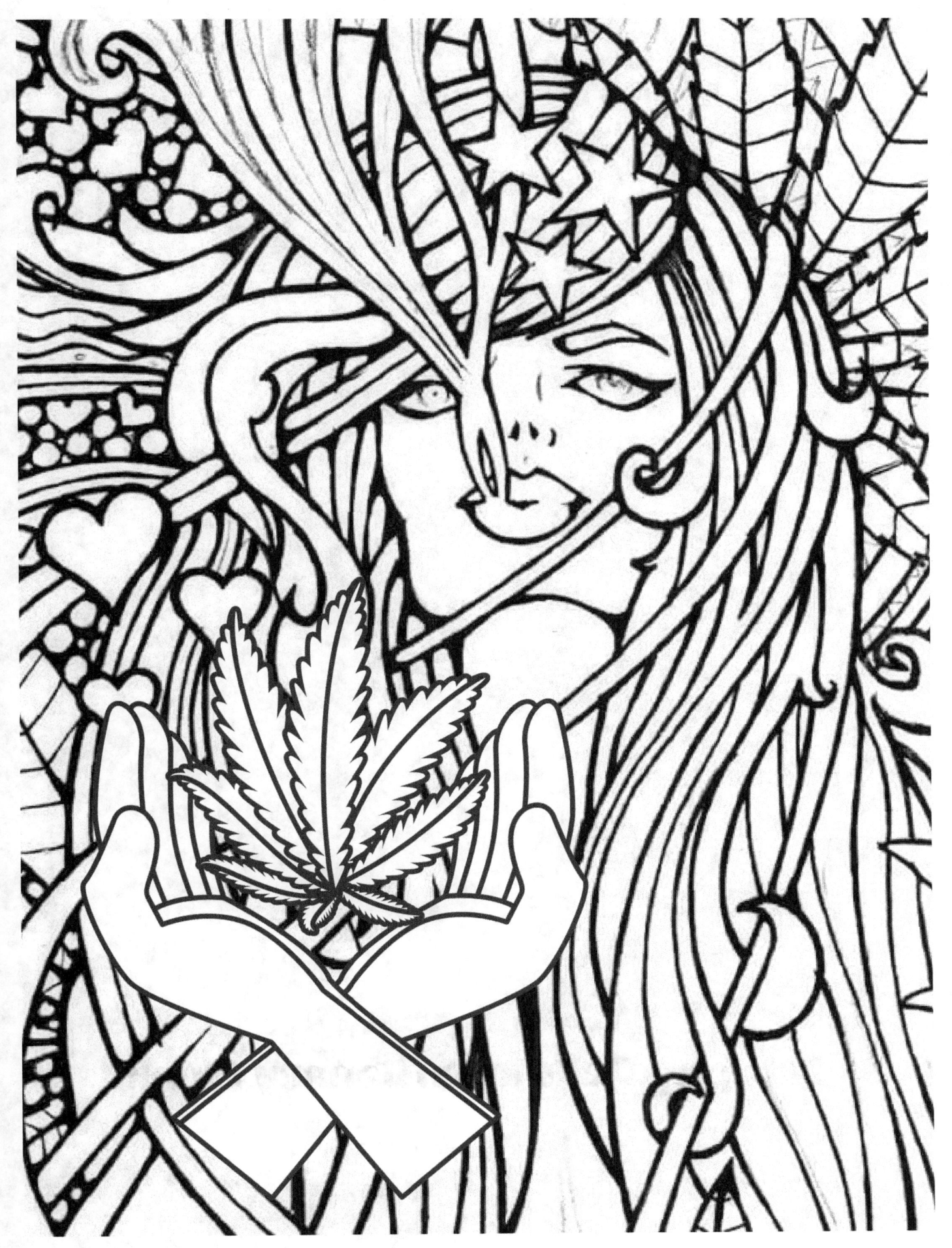

This page left intentionally blank.

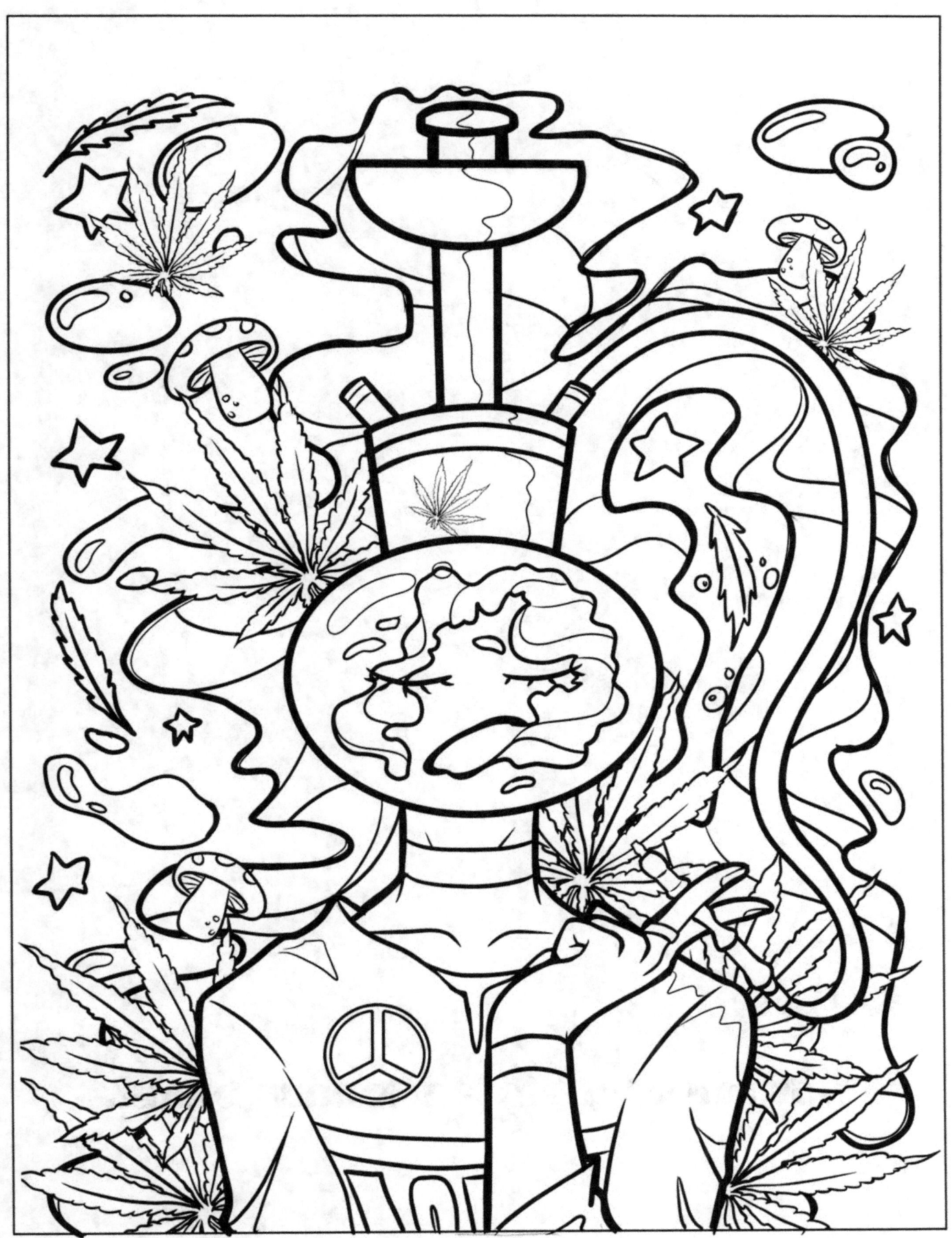

This page left intentionally blank.

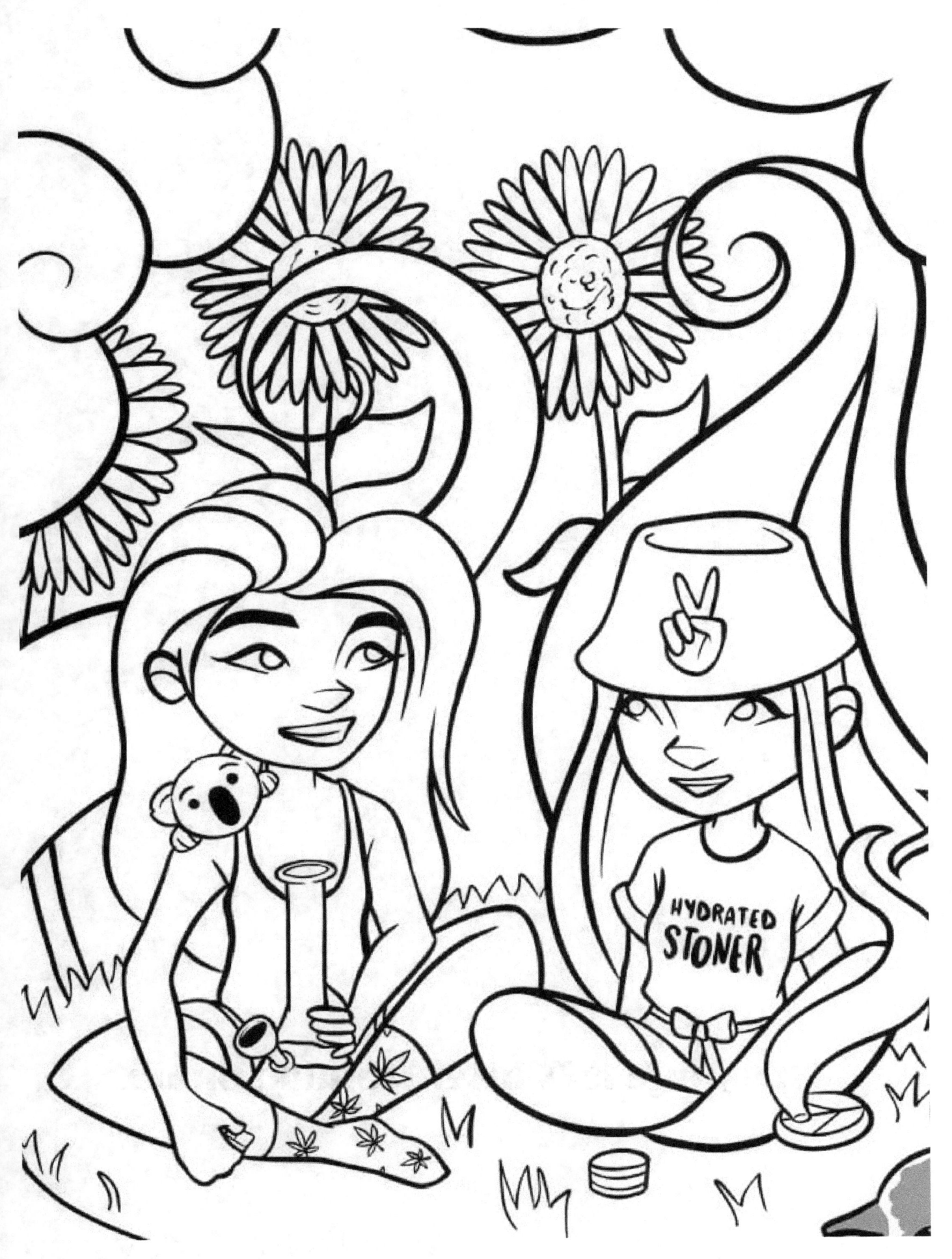

This page left intentionally blank.

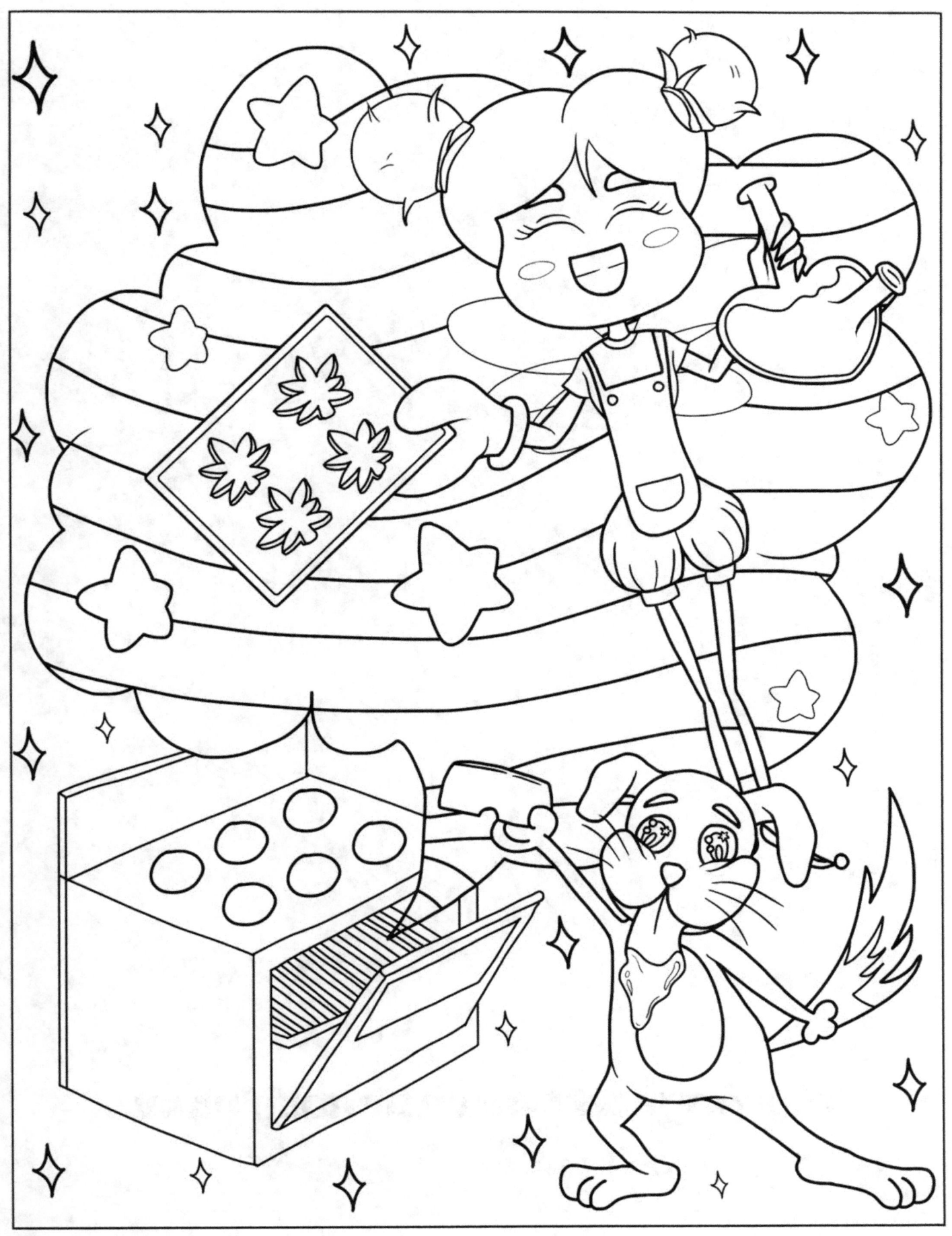

This page left intentionally blank.

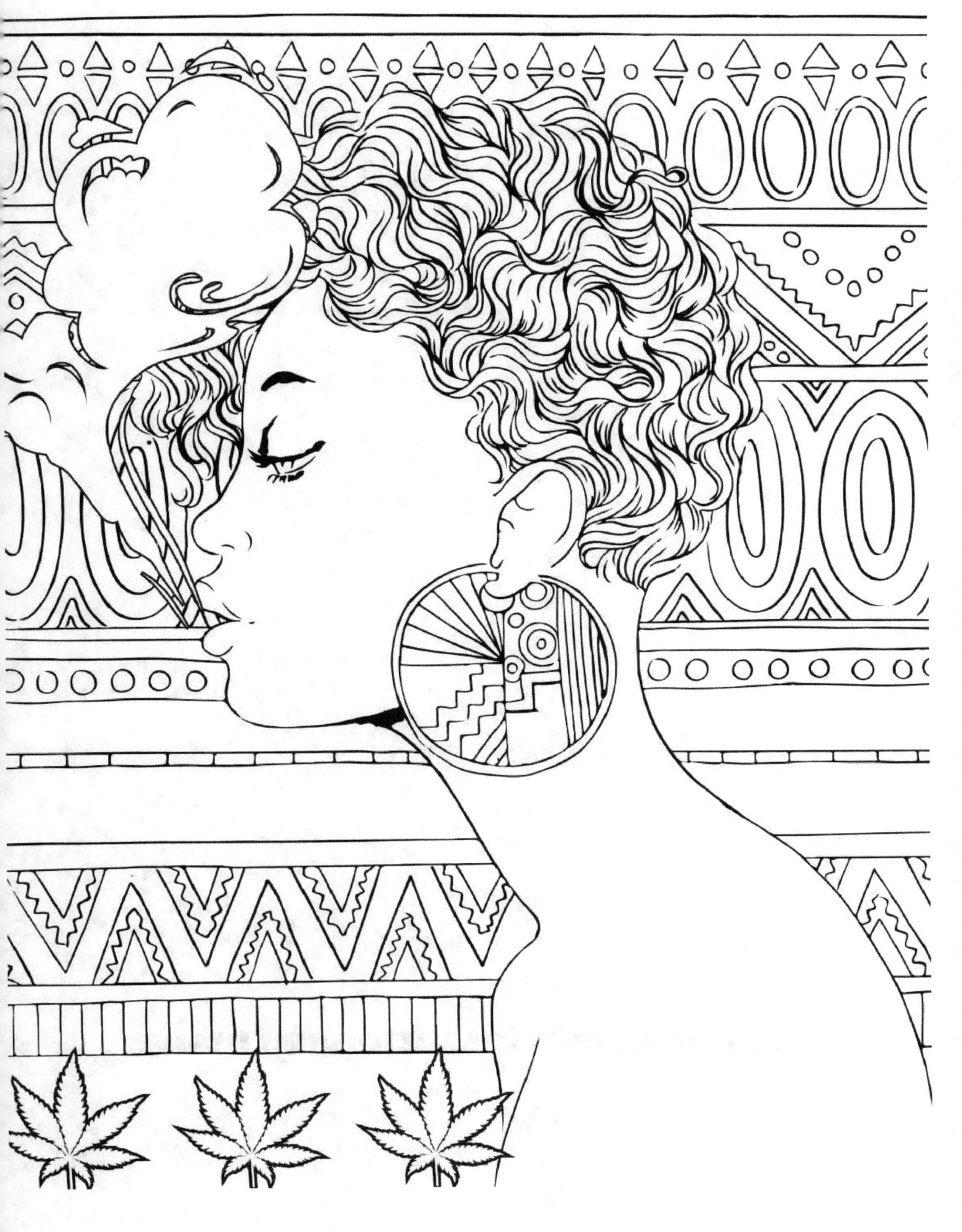

This page left intentionally blank.

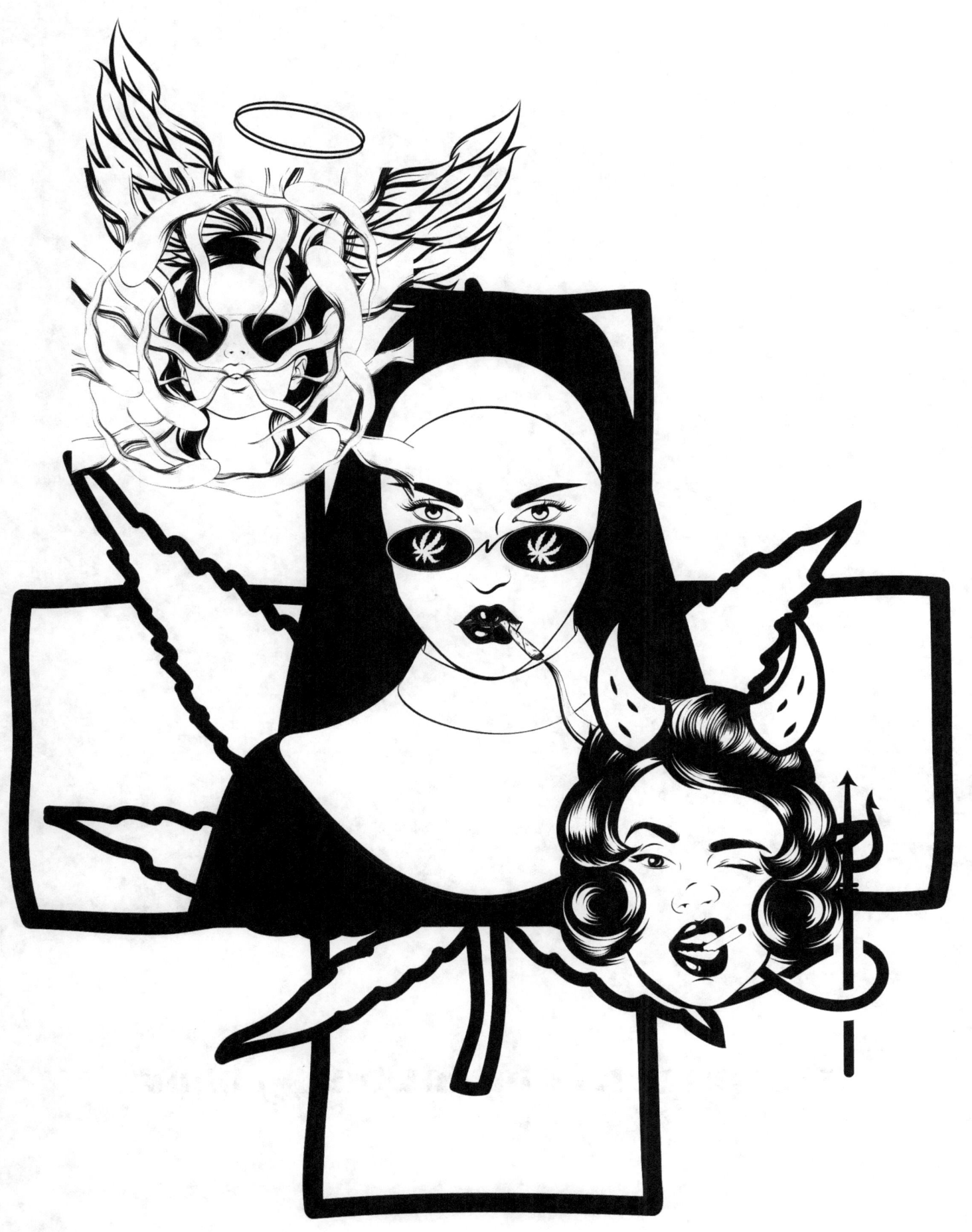

This page left intentionally blank.

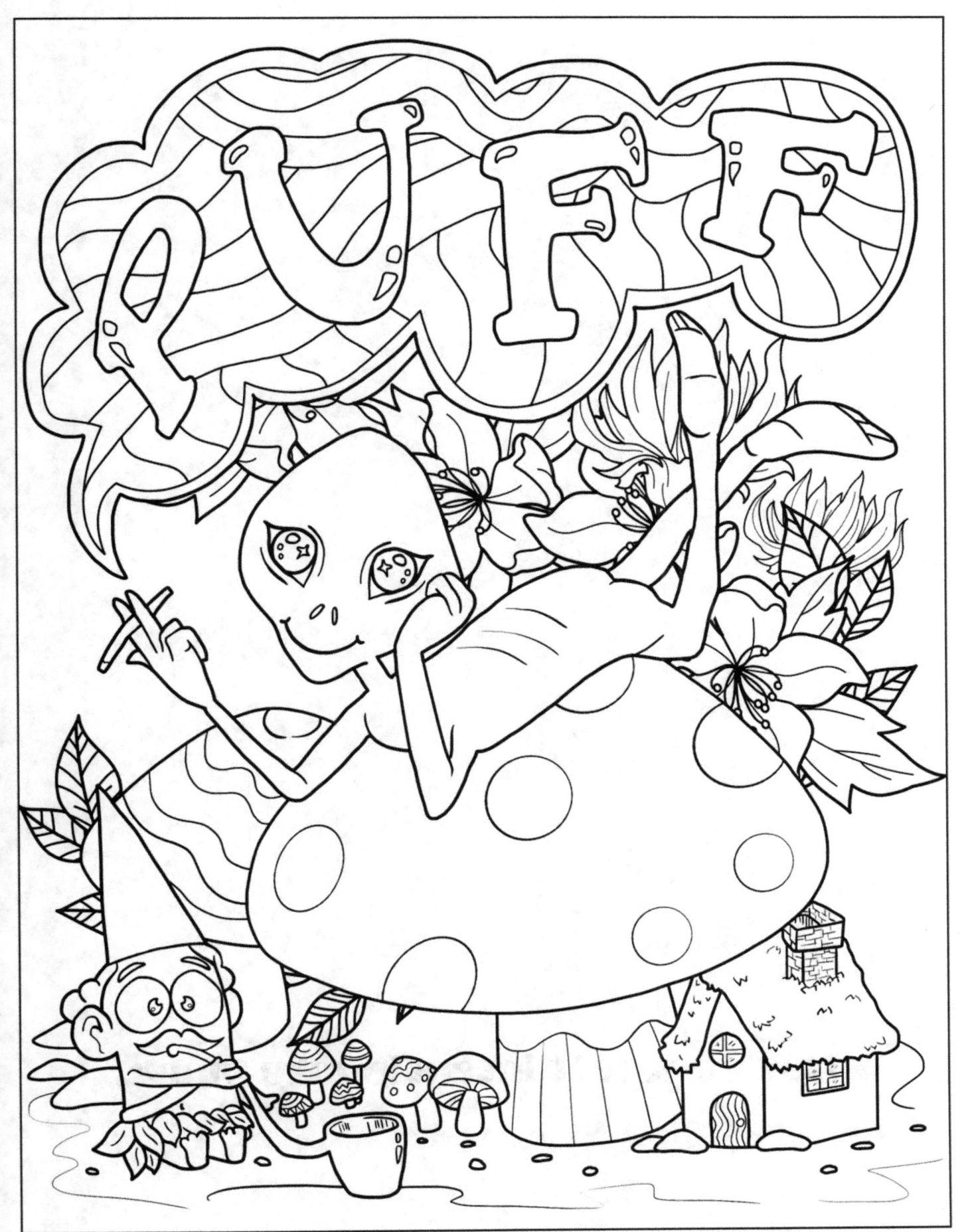

This page left intentionally blank.

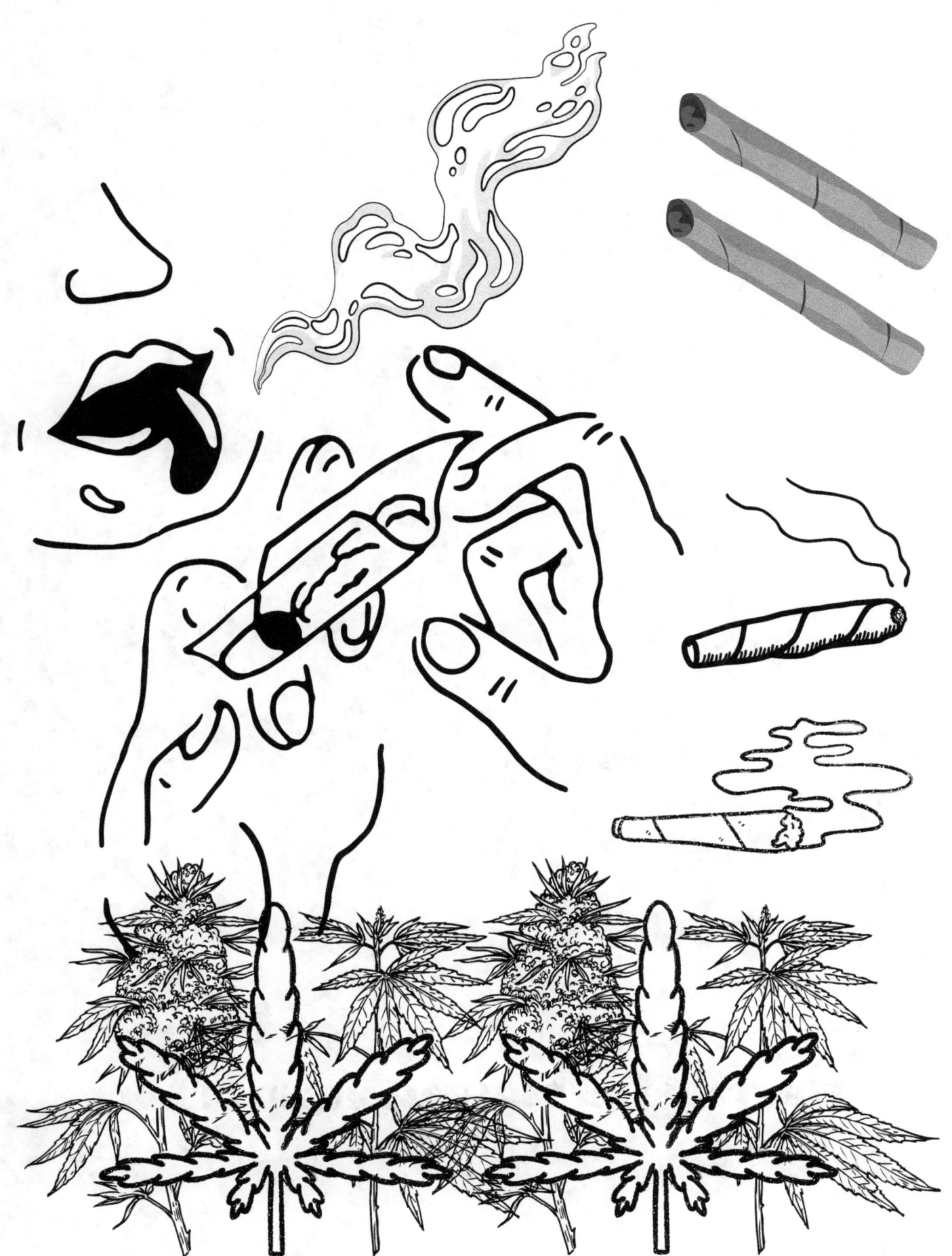

This page left intentionally blank.